AROUND THE WORLD IN SEARCH OF STEAM

Colin Garratt

AROUND THE WORLD IN SEARCH OF STEAM

DAVID & CHARLES
Newton Abbot   London   North Pomfret (Vt)

Acknowledgements

Heartfelt thanks to the many people who have made my work possible over the last twenty years whether through financial, moral or logistical support – they know who they are.

Thanks also to Julie Hunt and Bridget Gill for their untiring efforts on this manuscript; to Peter Thornton-Pett for his valuable guidance throughout, and to Liz Cole for contributing the delightful sketches.

Finally to my parents as I would never have began this self-imposed task without the stable upbringing they provided.

Contact

Parties offering support or liaison should contact Colin Garratt through Monica Gladdle who also handles all lectures and Audio-Visual enquiries/bookings. A Colin Garratt video cassette based on this book and entitled 'Around the World in Search of Steam' is also available. This 50-minute production in VHS and Beta (PAL and NTSC) depicts Colin at work around the world and brings to life many of the sentiments expressed within these pages.

Available from:
Monica Gladdle, Carlestrough Cottage, Shangton Road, Tur Langton, Leicestershire LE5 0PN (Tel: 085884 438)

Opposite title page: *At the childhood bridge in Newton Harcourt where the story begins.*

British Library Cataloguing in Publication Data

Garratt, Colin
    Around the world in search of steam.
    1. Locomotives – History
    I. Title
    625.2'61'0924   TJ603

    ISBN 0-7153-8550-X

Typeset by Typesetters (Birmingham) Ltd
Smethwick, West Midlands
and printed in Great Britain
by Redwood Burn Limited, Trowbridge, Wilts
for David & Charles Publishers plc
Brunel House   Newton Abbot   Devon

Published in the United States of America
by David & Charles Inc
North Pomfret .Vermont 05053   USA

Contents

How does one summarise the life enshrined within these pages? The question presupposes many conclusions and perhaps the matter should be settled in advance. And so when I die, inscribe my tombstone with the words 'A RAILWAYMAN' for I know of no greater honour.

·1·
Trainspotting and Childhood

The cab with its fiery incandescence was to my young eyes the furnace of Hell and, despite the beckoning of a benign fireman, I was terrified. The sound of the engine was ear-splitting; roaring and hissing with shrouds of steam. I was in a station at night and my parents wanted to lift me into the cab, convinced that I would enjoy it once aboard. They dragged me across the platform until my screams of anguish persuaded them otherwise, and I was allowed to stand awestruck at a safe distance. Perhaps my photographs owe something to subconscious images from childhood; certainly that fire-spitting monster made an indelible mark at an impressionable age.

That traumatic experience with a locomotive at night may have been on our Bournemouth holiday in 1946. Notice the wartime coastal defences still in place.

Trains played no further part in my life until I was nine when, one summer afternoon after school, a friend suggested a ride into the countryside on our new cycles. We left our village of Oadby and followed a track through the soft Leicestershire countryside until we arrived at a small village with a railway bridge. Leaning our bikes against the brickwork, we stood on our crossbars and gazed onto the shining tracks. After ten minutes a coal train came into sight. The engine was making a superb roaring sound and pumping grey smoke into the air. Mesmerised, I watched it approach until the engine's heavy exhaust became too frightening and we leapt from our crossbars. The smoke struck the bridge's underside and 'puthered' up in a mighty cloud. Another bridge was situated 200m – a quarter of a mile – along the line and, as we watched the engine forging its way towards it, we wondered whether the train would stretch between the two, and to our joy it did. This time feelings of fear had turned to wonder, and the evening represented a turning point in my life. I returned to that enchanted bridge on successive days and much of my remaining childhood was to be spent there.

The bridge was at Newton Harcourt, on the former Midland main line south

A Stanier 8F tackles the climb southwards through Newton Harcourt.

of Leicester. Every day of the summer holidays I cycled over, invariably alone, and sat on my own spot on the grassy bank until dusk, apart from occasional forays into the village for a bottle of apple crush and a wash at the communal pump. Sometimes I crossed the meadow to see the old coal barges passing on the Grand Union Canal, little realising that I was witnessing the end of the canal age. I stopped watching activities on the canal when they caused me to miss trains.

The surrounding countryside possessed a special wildness and beauty, so tranquil in those days before tourists and townspeople discovered it. A myriad of insects, birds, animals, flowers and giant thistles presented a diversity which was to mean almost as much to me as the railway. On fine evenings I would stay at Newton until dusk, waiting for the Burton-to-London beer trains, and the bats would be out before I started for home. The earth smelt sweet as I pedalled over the fields, and in the advancing twilight I could hear owls screeching, churring partridges and the clamour of rooks and jackdaws preparing to roost. The countryside became deeply ingrained as my birthright and, as with the trains, depredation was inconceivable.

During those post-war years it was difficult to obtain the now familiar ABC spotting books, so I wrote the engine numbers and names in a large red note-book. I still recall its red cover and my spidery writing; if I had that book today it would be one of my most treasured possessions.

Certain trains were still frightening, especially the railway officials' saloon which passed behind an old Midland Railway 2P 4-4-0, with 7ft-diameter driving wheels. It could be heard from more than a kilometre away, as for some reason the cylinder drains on the engine were always open and the tremendous roar of escaping steam was recognisable. Seeing this engine and one saloon coach with the bowler- and trilby-hatted officials inside was terrifying, and I would run from the embankment and duck down behind the hedge, returning only after the train had disappeared round the distant bend.

Britain's railways were the heartbeat of the nation's economy in 1949; more than twenty-five types of locomotive could be seen at my bridge, hauling trains of coal, iron ore, milk, beer, vegetables and fish, along with a fine variety of mixed freight. Passenger trains consisted of locals, semi-fasts and expresses. The most illustrious was the Thames–Clyde Express which ran from London (St Pancras) to Glasgow (St Enoch) via Leeds and Carlisle, whilst the least signifi-cant was the four-wagon 'Smelly Bone' which conveyed bones in open wagons from Leicester Cattle Market sidings to the glue factory near Market Harborough. This passed at lunchtime, and on hot days the stench of rotting bones would prevent me from eating my sandwiches until it had long passed.

My favourite locomotives were the LMS Jubilees with their Brunswick-green livery, tapered boilers, 6ft 9in-diameter driving wheels and brass nameplates glinting in the sun. Their syncopated three-cylinder beat as they tackled the climb southwards through Newton was as beautiful as any music, especially on summer evenings after rain. And how their names stimulated one's imagina-tion of Britain's legendary history; battles, generals, warships and our colonial possessions around the world; 191 in all – what patriotism they engendered *Malta GC, Nigeria, Gold Coast* – to name but a few. Here was the stuff of legends which harked back to the days when Britain was the premier country of the world. Those flamboyant engines merely confirmed what the teachers told us when they pointed to the map of the world, and said that the red areas – which seemed to cover at least one-third of the land mass – belonged to Britain. But the most important lesson of those early summers was an understanding of the railway as an institution of immeasurable pride; an efficient, energy conserving, safe and disciplined transport system, which served the country with a minimum of land usage and of environmental stress. Through the railway I began to understand the geography and economic structure of the country. Sitting on that grassy bank I sensed how the railway had made the Industrial Revolution possible, the centrifugal force of society itself. By the age of ten it was clear to me that railways were essentially right – the perfect form of land transport – a point in human evolution when the digits tallied – the jackpot in the gaming machine.

After eighteen months' initiation at Newton, I had seen most of the engines likely to pass and certainly all the types. The early 1950s heralded cycle trips to adjoining places, whilst for longer journeys we often used football excursion trains which offered cheap tickets. The most exciting cycle trip was to Rugby on

I grew up with the Jubilees, and Gwalior – a Leeds (Holbeck) engine – was a regular performer through Newton Harcourt on such trains as the Thames Clyde Express. She is seen here at Saxby in the company of Leicester driver Bernard Robinson collecting empty stock prior to working a women's hockey special from Leicester to Wembley. (David Smith)

the West Coast main line, which, in 1951, had a blissful variety of trains. The favourite spotting point was just south of the station where the Great Central crossed the West Coast main line by means of a girder bridge, overlooking the locomotive works, testing plant and shed. Here is a verbatim account from my notebook at the time.

RUGBY SHED AND WORKS TRIP. Mon 1st Nov 1954. It was our half term so I decided to go to Rugby for the day I caught the 8.47 stopping train for Rugby, from Leicester (London Rd). Our train left to time and after a quick journey Rugby (Midland) was reached on time. I then made my way to the shed and works. I reached the works, there was a few tenders outside but no locos. I opened the little works door at the front and walked in. Then I had a beautiful surprise there standing just to my left was CARR. DEPT. WOL No 7, I was overjoyed at seeing it. The engine had no chimney on, and I was later told it was waiting for a new one from Crewe. I had a good look round it and started looking for a works-plate with the help of a workman but we couldn't find one. He told me these engines which came out in 1870 used to shunt out in the big yards for the L.N.W.R. He said sometimes they came to Rugby instead of Crewe, and this one wants repair to its wheels. I myself had previously seen others of this class at Rugby. Also in the works was (which I copped) ex LNWR 0-8-0 49034 10D, 45304 10c, class 5MT 4-6-0. Others were 8F 2-8-0 48320, 2B 48175, 3A 48725, 3A and 5MT 4-6-0 No 45091 2E. Then I left the works and walked up to the loco shed in the shed I copped 49024 L.N.W.R. 0-8-0 off 8B and a 4F 0-6-0 No 44517 3D. I was very surprised to find two 14B class 5's on shed nos. 44825 and 45253. Now I made my way to the big Girder Bridge so I could also observe the L.N.E.R. trains as they passed over the top. I had another cop then it was class 5 4-6-0 no 45110 6J. Later I was told that a new 9F 2-10-0 92015 was in the testing plant bay. I walked round to the plant and entered the bay by a door in the side, and there it was; its tender was not coupled on to it. With the 9F stood a Crab 2-6-0. After returning to the Girders for a short time I went back to the Station. Standing at the head of the Leamington train was not the usual Ivatt 2MT 2-6-2T from 2C, but one from 8B. I asked the driver why 41322 8B was working the train and he said, well 41228 2C has gone to Horwich Works for an overhaul and 41322 8B has been sent down to replace it. I asked him if it was a good engine and he said yes I like it very much. Then he made some very sarcastic remarks about the old LNWR Webb 2-4-2T 46604 2C by saying all the men at Leamington longed to drive it, and all queued up to drive it, but he did agree 46604 had done well after its 64 years hard work (and still going). I spent the afternoon spotting on the station no very rare named engines were noted. 46244 King George V worked the southbound Royal Scot. Soon it was time to go and I crossed to where the 4.33 to Leicester stood. I had another cop before I left 70054 Dornoch Firth came in with an express. At 4.33 we got the right away and Leicester was reached on time. I had an amazing total of 9 cops, after a very enjoyable and interesting trip.

How sad for the youngsters of today who stand on the platform ends at Rugby watching the dreary and monotonous succession of electrics – the Great Central, of course, having long since been ripped up.

Trainspotting was breathtakingly exciting; the thrill of the unexpected loomed. In 1950 Britain had some 30,000 steam locomotives, embracing 600 different types, and no enthusiast worth his salt wanted to miss rarities when they appeared. With steam handling most of the nation's freight and a high percentage of passenger journeys too, the frequency of trains on the main lines ensured constant anticipation. Boys vied with each other in a quest to see all the members of a class. When a class was completed, it was said to be 'cleared'; withdrawn engines not seen were recorded as 'lost' and in railway works or on scraplines, where locomotives were likely to be found in pieces, frames were countable but interchangeable items like boilers and tenders were not.

The top Leicester spotter was Granny. He was older than the rest of us and held the rare distinction of having seen all but one of Stanier's 8Fs which totalled almost 700 engines. This was a considerable feat as most of us needed several dozen. Granny's last 8F was 48127 from Heaton Mersey, a Cheshire depot whose engines seldom worked southwards through the Midlands. However, one day during a routine afternoon's spotting the engine went through on a southbound freight. Fortunately Granny was not at the line that day, but in spite of our decision to say nothing, the news reached him within hours and we heard he had packed a rucksack, mounted his bicycle and pedalled furiously southwards, homing in on all the sheds south of Leicester, in the hope of running his last 8F to ground.

Such intense dedication was not exclusive to Granny; we were all as enthusiastic and I became an incorrigible 'bunker' – the term used for entering sheds and works without permission. Walls with broken-glass tops or barbed wire were small obstacles. We were often chased out, or caught and ejected by the depot foreman. A system of false names and addresses was evolved and written into our ABCs and notebooks to support the blatant lies we told. One of my favourite addresses was 3 Adam and Eve Street, Market Harborough, the unlikeliness of which was its own plausibility. The street actually exists and I often wondered what the beleaguered occupants of that house did when every couple of months or so the police came knocking. Little less plausible was my assumed name, Harold Coils. 'C-O-Y-L-E-S?' I can still hear angry officials snapping; 'No, C-O-I-L-S', I would reply politely. Many of the trips were nothing short of full-blooded adventures. We would bunk sheds all day and sleep in the carriage sidings at night – in first-class compartments if we could find them.

Our seriousness occasionally gave way to unbridled bouts of bad behaviour. Our most regular spotting haunt was The Birdcage, a walkway that overlooked Leicester's Midland shed yard. The Birdcage was enclosed on one side by wire meshed girders and on the other by the wall of Hillcrest, a former Victorian workhouse that had been converted into a dismal institution for the old and mentally sick. In the intervals between trains we would stretch precariously over the wire in order to drop heavy objects onto the roof of the yard controller's wooden hut situated forty feet below. He was a crusty character we called 'Dad' and the resounding 'thwack' of our missiles projected onto his tarpaulined roof never failed to create the desired reaction. The sight of him ridden by anger as he stood shouting up at us, with bulging eyes and shaking fist, was our ample reward.

Another nasty habit was played upon unsuspecting boys who would turn up at The Birdcage, lean their bikes against the wall and focus their attention on the railway below. Several of us would engage one of these innocent boys in conversation, asking him what he had seen and looking through his ABC whilst another group would dismantle his bike, sometimes down to almost every individual component – including removal of tyres and inner tubes – whereupon we would move away from our victim one by one and wait until he saw his bike carefully laid out in pieces on the pavement, whereupon a little fellow named Umpleby delivered his classic line, 'Aye up, son, beats me how you got here on that'.

But such behaviour paled to insignificance as my spotting trips spread further afield, and I witnessed the blackened remains of the Industrial Revolution in South Wales, Lancashire, North East England and Glasgow. The stark landscape with grimy streets, slag heaps, endless factories and belching chimneys made almost as deep an impression upon me as had the railway. Britain was the workshop of the world, and I had seen that workshop before it was tidied up and, in later years, largely closed down. So immersed was I in a legendary past that the 11-plus fell by the wayside. I sat in the classroom on the examination day, whispering to a companion that I was too young to have such responsibility fostered upon me. Failure was inevitable.

Despairing, my parents sent me to a private school in Leicester where, they hoped, improved discipline would correct some of my aberrations. Events proved otherwise; my immediate rebellion against compulsory sport found me ostracised and alone each Wednesday afternoon to do specially set lessons in an empty school. The best thing I achieved there was to set up a railway society which, apart from having a thriving membership, was active on weekend visits all over the country. Once the school day ended, it was down to the local sheds; the Midland, Great Central or Great Northern. The Midland was the favourite with eighty-five engines allocated, ranging from superannuated inside-cylinder 0-6-0s to newly built Standard 5s from Derby Works. The Great Central and the Great Northern, though smaller, held a completely different range of classes. The Central had Gresley A3s, including 'Flying Scotsman', whilst my instincts for historical locos were nurtured by the Great Northern where I savoured seeing J6 and J5 0-6-0s which worked in from Colwick along with Ragtimer K2s.

61945.   53A.
Carlton (way home)

62053   31B.   62

Monday 26th July.
64420 38A Leicester GN shed.
Tuesday 27th July.
42882. 68A   Kingmoor.
61271.   38A Central Shed
61125.   36A Central Station

Wednesday 28th July
61142 40B   10-10 - Birmingham.
Thursday 29th July
       Rugby
45182 10C Rugby Works.
46483 27A Rugby Works.
45409 12A Rugby Works.
49419 8A Rugby Shed
61434 50A Girder Bridge (ex works light)
49375 8A Near Testing Plant at Rugby.
48705 3A Southbound Freight.
90538 36A Southbound Freight.
90039 38E Girder Bridge (travelling at
almost 60MPH on a passenger train.)

42575 9A Light under Girder
Bridge from Station
Friday 30th July
49557 26A. Leicester Yard
(first Fowler 7F, later took 2-35
goods to Wellingbro'.)
43620. 21A. Leicester Yard.
61418. 50A York Goods.
48089. 9F Leicester Yard.

Saturday 31st July.
63659. 3iC Central Shed.
62059. 51C Central Shed.
Wednesday 4th August.
64385 36E Mkt Harborough Shed
Thursday 5th August.
78029 15C Leicester (seen arriving)
Friday 6th August.
45416 12A double heading a jubilee
at Rugby.
13052 NYA Coupled to a Consol
on a goods train at Rugby (to south
Saturday 7th August.
48473 20C Last Royston consol

A page from my trainspotting diary of 1954. Only the 'Cops' (engines never seen before) are recorded. These were the days when trainspotting was as exciting as great football.

Certain special workings on the Central came in every evening bringing interesting or potentially rare types. Often we rushed down to the fish dock to see the Great Western Hall from Banbury, and be back again by 8.30pm, when the 'York goods' would arrive, frequently behind one of the beautiful B16 4-6-0s. Later, at dusk, we would visit The Birdcage to see the broccoli specials running during the vegetable season, bringing the promise of rare Central Division 4Fs. These activities used to keep us until after ten o'clock at night, homework having been sacrificially abandoned. The magnetic pull of the railway was irresistible; locomotives were not inanimate objects, built for a purpose; they were living personalities of their own and all were different. However many engines there were within a class, we saw them as individuals.

Whatever my education suffered in conventional learning was more than compensated for by my travels; I knew the geography of my country better than most adults, and by the age of fifteen had visited almost every town in Britain. It was an idyllic adolescence as the mid-fifties was a period of great stability, and to my dying day I will believe that the absoluteness of our railway was one of the pillars of that stability. Then, like a bolt from the blue, tragedy struck one morning in 1955 when my father showed me the headline in our national newspaper: the modernisation plan for railways, under which steam traction was to be phased out. But steam engines were as permanent as the streets upon which we walked; they certainly wouldn't disappear just because the government had drawn up a plan. Even if it were true, it was bound to take ten times longer than the government said. Everyone at the lineside agreed, so we didn't worry.

Looking back, I regret that I didn't use a camera more fully. I did take a few black and white pictures during those years, and some survive, but what a wealth of visual images I let slip through my fingers – trainspotting being infinitely more important. Little did I guess that the end of the steam age was the event which plotted my future. Had I known, life might have been simpler, for I was fifteen and under pressure to decide upon a career. My parents came from what they called working class backgrounds, my father having begun work at fourteen as, in his words, 'a scruffy kid with a hole in his trousers, sweeping the factory floor'. That he rose to be a member of the board of one of Britain's leading clothing manufacturers was due to sheer hard work and determination to get on. Naturally he looked to his son to do the same.

The threats were legion; I would end up as a dustman or a spotty-faced clerk. The situation was worsened by a succession of bad school reports. It was farcical for my parents to go on paying for my education; so at fifteen I left, and, bereft of any better notion, took a job in an insurance office. A year later, still without direction, logic dictated that I should work on the railway and, in 1956, I joined BR as a clerk in offices at the Midland shed in Leicester, overlooked by The Birdcage itself.

·2·
Railways, Jazz and Commerce

Now I was on the inside looking out! It was paradise to be working amongst the engines, and half the movements in the depot yard went immediately past our office window, totally dwarfing the building and causing the ground to tremble. There were eight of us on the clerical staff, working under a chief clerk, and our office was situated next to those of the running shed foreman and shed-master. My duties centred upon calculating on the men's time cards the total hours worked, taking into consideration overtime, night work, Sundays and rest days. Also, the locomotive distance had to be calculated from the driver's

View from The Birdcage overlooking Leicester Midland depot. The coaling tower is on the left whilst our offices can be seen in the background. Our Midland Simples are in store although a Jinty had just been returned from overhaul at Derby Works (rear right). (M. Mitchell)

daily duty sheets. These were forwarded to Derby HQ, and used in the totalling of distance for routine examination and shopping. Sometimes I was sent on relief to other depots, and my favourite was Wellingborough. The journey was made on a London express worked by a top-link Leicester crew and invariably I was able to travel on the footplate over the fifty-four kilometres. The engine was usually a Black 5, the type that has gone down in railway history as probably Britain's best allround design, and we would burst beneath the bridge at Newton Harcourt at speeds faster than a mile a minute (96km/h).

Being part of the railway confirmed my belief in its greatness. Pride and skill were pre-eminent; it was a vast and challenging industry which moulded the characters of the workers within it. The responsibility of running a service which was the nation's lifeline was a source of great pride to the men. It was not a job but a way of life. Clocking on at 2.18am in pouring rain, confronted with a rundown 8F and a tender full of bed coal was all part of the challenge.

They knew the locomotive not as a machine but as a living thing which – like a horse – needed to be coaxed and encouraged in order to give of its best. Such was the insular nature of the industry that the men became lost within it – and events which occurred outside were of little significance. The irregular routine forbade social activities unless in connection with the job, but for many men the job was sufficient. Romance, music and the arts did not feature in their daily lives; the engines were their women, and intense emotional energy was channelled into the job. Affection, companionship and honour were ever-prevalent and beneath all the carping and ribaldry the men cared for each other. Theirs was a common challenge, a common danger, and each worker was respected for the role he played. Many of the men were almost legends in their own time, and invariably nicknamed in accordance with long industrial tradition. One of my first encounters with this was a much disliked shedman known to everyone as 'Treacle' because, I was told – without the slightest flicker of humour – 'he's a sticky bastard'. A more lovable character was Bedtick Smith, who had a curious affection for his overcoat. Day and night he wore it, summer and winter, and when asked why he wore it during the hot weather, always replied, 'What keeps cold out keeps 'eat out'. Rumour has it that when Bedtick died, the coat had to be removed with a blowlamp.

A character from further back in time whose legend remains, was the Sandrat, said to have lived in the depot's sandhole. He was small, wiry, and had no fixed address. He is said to have stored his money in a St Bruno tobacco tin. One night the Sandrat was run down and killed by an engine and the sandhole was searched for the tin, but it was never found, and to this day, half a century later, if a Leicester Division man is seen

The Sandrat.

to have more money than usual he faces the inevitable question, 'What yer done? Found the Sandrat's tin?'

One driver not so popular with his mates was 'Firebright' Townsend who was notorious for his heavy driving, causing so much fire and sparks that housewives would pull their washing in whenever he was booked to pass. Bank fires were his speciality and the local fire brigades as far north as Leeds knew him well.

Tommy Godfrey – doing a turn for the lads.

Tommy Godfrey was the greatest joker of all. 'More like Trinder than Trinder', Tommy had an inexhaustible repertoire of practical jokes to be used on any unsuspecting victim. A favourite was his 'Which way' routine which shattered many a poor man's faith in railways. During trips to London, while in a station, Tommy would lean out of his cab and, beckoning to the nearest person on the platform – often a father showing his son the engine – would shout, 'S'cuse me, mate, d'you live 'ere?' If the hapless parent replied in the affirmative, Tommy would lean forward and whisper, 'Is this the right way to London?' Once, after working a football special down to St Pancras, Tommy turned up at the Kentish Town foreman's office to report for orders with a patch over his eye, prompting them to ring Leicester depot to find out what one of their men was doing working a main line train with only one eye. Sometimes Tommy would saw the end off a shunting pole and put the hook under his sleeve to obtain a similar response from officials at other sheds.

It was the magnitude of the industry, and its role as the nation's lifeline that enabled such characters to evolve. The railway – like religion – was bigger than man; the challenge of the operations and maintenance of safety brought out the best in them and engendered a team spirit rare today. It was without doubt Britain's greatest industry.

My absorption in railways did not preclude an awareness of the social change that swept the nation during the fifties; the emancipation of the young who, in the grip of rock and roll fever, were experiencing new emotions, inevitably had its effects, and conversation on railway trips became divided between engines and music. My own interests gravitated towards traditional New Orleans jazz; several railway friends shared my enthusiasm and we made visits to the Ken Colyer Club off the Charing Cross Road, both for Saturday evening and all night sessions. We travelled down by train from Leicester behind a Jubilee or a Britannia. The latter were especially exciting as one could invariably count upon a 160km/h sprint over the racing ground between Bedford and Luton. The all night sessions were magic; the jazz was exciting, yet breathtakingly beautiful, and the atmosphere characterised the relaxed timelessness of the fifties. Some weekends, Ken played the club on Sunday evening too, and I often stayed over in London. Once, with time to spare on the Sunday afternoon, I went to the club early. A group was playing to an audience of seven people, at least three of whom were the band, but their early rhythm-and-blues style intrigued me. On leaving, I made a point of finding out what they were called. Their name was The Rolling Stones.

Now for the first time in my life I had some idea of what I wanted to do – to become a professional musician – and along with several of my railway friends formed a band, with me on trumpet. But music didn't come easy. Long hours had to be spent practising, including lunchtimes down at the sheds, where the only suitable place was in the office toilets. Railwaymen take most things in their stride, but this was a new experience. My raucous exhalations, amplified by the brick buildings, could be heard all over the depot; retribution was inevitable. One day, as I sat on the toilet in a locked closet blowing my head off, a handful of oily cotton waste from the fitting shop was ignited and pushed under the door of the adjacent washroom. Eventually the blue smoke became unbearable but upon opening the door of the closet I was confronted with a dense acrid fog in the washroom. Choking, I flung myself in vain against the locked outer door. Suffocation was averted only by opening the small toilet window through which, gasping and red-faced, I emerged head first to land in a heap on the ground outside to the sheer joy of at least fifty onlookers. Thenceforth endeavours to play like Bunk Johnson were conducted away from the railway.

Parental pressure to take up a 'serious' career precluded both railways and music, and in 1957 I took the opportunity to become a trainee sales representative with a wholesale grocery company. Besides a steady income came the advantage of a company car, which could be used at weekends for railway trips. Now for the first time I began to take pictures in deference to the changes being wrought on the railway system.

Britain's last steam locomotive had been built in 1960, and although the writing was clearly on the wall, most people believed that steam would last out the century. But the steam age was declining more rapidly than I realised, so great was my immersion in music. The band was playing well and we soon opened our own club called The Broken Drum in Leicester city centre, playing there every Sunday night. We developed a following; the music got better, and other bookings came in. The nights were late and sometimes I only just had time to drive home and change before calling on my first customer. I held my job down well enough but inevitably my bleary-eyed sluggishness and increasingly late arrivals for work began to cause the management concern, and several times I was called into the sales director's office to be told that I must decide between my career or the 'dance band', as he irreverently called it.

Leading the Superior Band. Emotions which would have been expressed through the bell of a trumpet have since come out in my photography.

It was at this time that I met the first of three Judys who were to exert a profound influence upon future events. Judy Maddock was the sixteen-year-old sister of our bass player and, from the first time I saw her, I knew she was a natural jazz singer and asked her to join the band. She quickly developed a feeling for the blues; her intonation was black and she sang – and looked – like Bessie Smith. Even her spirituals were 'Saturday Night Blues dressed up for Sunday morning', whilst her treatment of up-tempo numbers like 'Wish I could shimmy like my sister Kate', was spine-tingling. The Broken Drum Club served coffee at the end of the evening and I would tell Cecilia, the manageress, to take the milk outside until after Judy's last set, or her shimmering blue tonalities would turn it sour.

By 1965, tensions within the firm came to a head whilst musically we had reached an impasse; I wanted to take the whole band to London and turn professional but none of them – apart from Judy – was prepared to take the risk. A decision had to be made and the music won; I left the firm and with money saved bought a Sunbeam Talbot. It was autumn 1965; Judy and I left the Superior Band, loaded our belongings into the car, and set off for London. The journey took in a two-week stopover in the New Forest in order to pay respect to the last steam expresses in Britain which were running from London (Waterloo), to Southampton, Bournemouth and Weymouth. I photographed assiduously during that fortnight mainly from within the forest around Brockenhurst. The golden sunlight heightened the beauty of a flaming autumn yet it was in many ways a deeply sad time; finally the realisation had come that steam trains were going to disappear as surely as had many of the great jazzmen we admired. The surviving New Orleans men were aged and it seemed that every month *Melody Maker* would report the death of yet another. The two things I cared most about were on the point of extinction.

Upon reaching London we took accommodation in Clapham, each of us having a tiny flat in a house run by an enormous Maltese landlady with a hot temper. She was not kindly disposed to musicians coming in during the early hours, but her best vitriol was reserved for our trombonist, John Williams, who used to sleep on the floor of my room when we played late. Some sixth sense always told her when he was in the house and she would prowl the hall and stairways hoping to catch him as he tried to creep out before breakfast. There were some dreadful shindigs over this, and one of the funniest sights I have ever seen was John running up the garden path carrying his trombone case with our landlady in hot pursuit wielding a huge carpet-beater.

The thrill of having our name set alongside 'The Guvenor's' makes this 1963 press clipping one of my most treasured possessions.

We used to rehearse the band in a room over a pub in W8, frequented by transvestites. One of them took a liking to our music and would often engage me in conversation. It was my first encounter with transvestism and I remember the desperate effort I made to react normally to a rugged labourer wearing a blond curly wig, lipstick, powder and a fur coat. Railway preoccupation at this time had subsided somewhat, although we did go to Clapham Junction to watch the expresses on the main line from Waterloo. During this period was an unforgettably sad day when I travelled on the last steam train from Paddington, hauled by No 7029, *Clun Castle*. Tear-

During our stay in the New Forest we often visited Eastleigh sheds and here is Judy Maddock with Callington, a Bournemouth Pacific which survived until the end of Southern steam.

stained faces lined the route all the way down to the West Country as *Clun's* mournful whistle drifted through the countryside.

Exciting though London was, it became obvious that making a living from music was impossible. The strict New Orleans style was not appealing commercially; beat groups and discos were rapidly taking over; jazz clubs were closing as fast as the steam depots. Penniless and frustrated, Judy and I returned to Leicester in 1966, and to the chagrin of my parents I returned home unemployed. I was 26 and – as I was never allowed to forget – most of my contemporaries from school were already married and established in proper careers.

The following months were confined to railway photography until one evening the phone rang. My former boss from the grocery company was offering a new job; he'd heard that I was back home and, assuming that the music bug had been blown out of my system, offered me the position of sales manager of the catering division. I accepted, and, exactly one year after leaving, I was back with a promotion that I almost certainly would not have received had I never left; the moral of this has fascinated me ever since. Now, with a good income, a company car and a regular working week, I was able to make frequent forays to areas where steam survived.

Shortly before steam ended I made the transition from black and white photography to colour. This was occasioned by a friend projecting his slides onto the wall of my flat. Colour slides were not common in the mid sixties, and the drama of those huge images in all their colourful luminosity engendered a feeling of actually being a part of the picture, and their effect was hypnotic. Next day I bought my first roll of slide film.

My early colour pictures were taken on the Southern, and many happy Saturdays were spent at Worting Junction, where the Bournemouth and West of England lines diverged, and one could lie on the grassy banks listening to the Bulleid Pacific's glorious three-cylinder rhythms. Worting's rural charm contrasted with Basingstoke Station, a fine location for speed. The screaming whistle of the expresses as they approached and the way in which they roared through the station at speeds of up to 144km/h, shaking the building and lifting newspapers from the bookstalls, is unforgettable. The steam age's last great fling was being played out in epic manner and, during those final years, speeds of 160km/h and more were being recorded with increasing regularity by crews conscious of the traditions they were ending.

Everyone dreaded the day that the Southern would finish and when the final Sunday came, in May 1967, all remaining locomotives were dispatched to Nine Elms, Weymouth, or Salisbury for disposal. On that fateful evening I stopped at Salisbury and found the shed crammed with engines, most of which had come in light or coupled together in pairs that day. All fires had been dropped but the engines were still in steam. It was an eerie and unforgettable experience, for the shed was alive with the hissings and gurglings of the dying locomotives. We continued our long journey home in complete silence.

The final months of British steam were confined to Lancashire, where the last Stanier 8Fs and Black 5s eked out their working lives on secondary duties; they were unkempt, rundown, with steam leaking from every joint. It was a harrowing end to a great epoch, until the day came in August 1968 when BR dropped the last fire to extinguish the Industrial Revolution's brightest light.

It seemed as if the backbone of progress had been removed; Britain had rejected her greatest technological gift to the world. Then, like a thunderbolt, it struck me; wouldn't other nations do the same? Weren't high-investment companies already geared to diesel production, and committed to the doctrine that steam was dirty, inefficient, outmoded and anti-social? Were not oil interests a dominating force in commercial and political life? The entire heritage would have disappeared by the end of the century. Surely a meaningful pictorial record, in one properly co-ordinated library should be made, capturing the final years of the epoch on modern colour transparencies. In so

The final months of steam traction in Britain were especially harrowing. Depots became cluttered with condemned engines waiting to be towed to breakers' yards as in this scene at Trafford Park.

doing I would evoke the memories from twenty years of watching trains, injecting the rhythms and colours from my musical training; in effect, bringing jazz into visual form. Intellectually the concept was perfect, but it was practically defective. There were no funds for such a venture and, having failed once with music, it was even more logical to fail as a railway photographer.

But a catalyst appeared in the form of the second Judy, an introspective sprig of a girl with yellow hair and a pre-Raphaelite aura. Judy Warner was ambitious, artistic and adventurous; she had a keen visual sense and, impressed by my pictures, urged me to abandon the futile existence of selling groceries, and to put the dream into action. In pursuit of her aims, Judy invested time, money and emotion. Her perseverance finally won and on Friday, 31 August 1969, I handed in the company's car, locked my office, and said goodbye to my secretary. My boss drove me home to a tiny suburban bedsitter taken in readiness to begin the task. With a warm handshake, my chief wished me well, but the guarded look in his eyes indicated many forebodings as to my future well-being. Standing on the pavement, watching his car disappear, mixed emotions welled up; I had slammed the door on a promising career and rejected commerce in favour of an aesthetic ideal; but the break was made and for the second time I turned to the railway for a career.

'There'll be a hot time in the old town tonight.' Colin Garratt's Superior Jazz Band with Judy Maddock. Casino Ballroom, Leicester 1964.

·3·
Professional on £4.50 a week

Rent day was Friday.

The bedsit was tawdry, one of ten in an ornate nineteenth-century house owned by an ageing review girl from Broadway. My weekly income was a meagre £4.50 obtained from social security; the rent was £3, leaving little for food and electricity. But I was still young, potentially on the threshold of an exciting new career, and Leicester's Clarendon Park – a miniature Chelsea – was the perfect breeding ground from which to begin my task.

Rent day was Friday and the landlady unashamedly clasping a black swag bag, drew up in a bright blue Daimler that half filled the street. On all but the hottest days she wore furs, hideously out of place amid the peeling paintwork and linoleum floor. The mere sight of her was enough to incite rebellion. There were several ways to retaliate; a favourite being the replacement of light bulbs on stairways and landings that had been illuminated to a foggy yellow gloom by miserable 15-watt lamps. These blew regularly, occasionally on the day when they were inserted, plunging the hall and stairs into darkness, and I would buy 100-watt Osrams in replacement, deducting the money from the rent. The luxury of those Osrams really put us back into the twentieth century, but the landlady's howls of anguish over the extra cost could be heard all over the house as, wringing her hands in despair, she held the swag bag aloft in Shakespearian tragedy.

But such jocularities were tempered by a determination to succeed. A close friend had given me six months, 'You'll be back to the firm cap in hand yet', he said, 'no one has ever made a living photographing trains – not to mention going all over the world to do it; you have no funds, no decent camera, and neither are you any great shakes as a photographer; the whole idea is untenable'. His words could not be dismissed easily, and the anxieties I felt manifested when my hair began to fall out. I sought help, only to be told by 'experts' at Leicester trichology clinic that the loss would continue if not treated. And the cost? £150 for six sessions. My heart sank; I couldn't pay. Fortunately the problem solved itself once my nervous system acclimatised to the challenge, and I quickly got down to the first task, to document the last Northamptonshire Ironstone Railways.

This industry, which had been host to vast numbers of working locomotives, was threatened due to the incredible economics that made it cheaper to convey higher grade ore from overseas. Many of these trips were made with the late Rev Teddy Boston, who was celebrated for having the Cadeby Light Railway

The Rev 'Teddy' Boston sharing the fascination of steam railways with young visitors to Cadeby Rectory as Teddy's wife Audrey looks on. (Coventry Evening Telegraph)

running through his rectory grounds, but who was locally notorious for under-taking shopping trips to nearby Market Bosworth on his traction engine. Teddy, a rotund jovial figure, belonged to the Wessex novels and, being with him in such beautiful settings as Cranford and Storefield, recalled a forgotten England. But his joyful eccentricities did little to conceal a deep faith, for Teddy was the personification of the Christian ethic. He put on monthly 'steaming days' for friends and visitors, followed by slide shows and fish and chip suppers in the rectory and it was at these events that I gave my first slide lectures.

Our lovely excursions to the Northamptonshire Ironstone Railways were short lived. By 1970 Nassington was the only system with steam traction, with its two Hunslet 16in 0-6-0 saddle tanks named *Jacks Green* and *Ring Haw* after two local woods. I regularly hitched out to Nassington through the warm autumn days of 1969 with my camera and lunch in a canvas rucksack. The quarry was situated in deep countryside; wild strawberries grew by the trackside and the trains would flush out pheasants from the lineside woods. It was a harmonious combination of industry and nature, the distant sound of the working engines mingled with the rumble of operations in the quarry. Huge diggers lifted the fragmented ore from the bed of a vast gullet and once the wagons were loaded the little Hunslets left in a storm of drama, bound for the connection with British Rail.

By Christmas a fair range of pictures had been amassed, and the first intrepid step in my new career was to have a book published. As O. S. Nock was, and still is, the world's most prolific railway author, I decided to ring him from the phone box around the corner from my bedsit. Having collected a huge pile of coins, I nervously dropped them into the slot as we spoke. Amazingly, he invited me to visit his office at the Westinghouse Company in Bath, of which he was a director. He was impressed with the pictures and agreed to give me an introduction to the Blandford Press.

'Write to them', he said, 'and I will send a covering letter to arrive before yours'. I did so, and fervently awaited a reply. When the crisp white envelope finally arrived, it carried an invitation to lunch to discuss a possible book and I was asked to bring a selection of pictures for examination; these were scrutinised under a huge magnifying glass. The meeting went better than my wildest dreams; £500 was offered as an outright fee for 150 colour pictures and 30,000 words of text. £500! Enough to finance an expedition! Arriving home that night I ran up the stairs three at a time just as the chap from the flat above was coming down. 'You look as if you've won a fortune!' he said. 'I have!' I told him as I flung open my door and danced wildly around the little room. It was December 1969, and less than four months after leaving the firm, the contract for my first book had been signed.

Money was still short, but with the help of artist David Weston, who had also just made the break and turned professional, I undertook to teach three twelve-

Happy days at Nassington with Jacks Green *and* Ring Haw *seen here in the gullet. Notice the fragmented ore bed in the foreground.*

week photographic courses at three different adult education centres in order to supplement my earnings. Each lesson demanded concentrated research and, although the money was welcome, the greatest benefit of those classes was to meet Monica. She was the wife of a Leicester knitwear manufacturer and had recently left the family business and adopted photography as a hobby. She was vivacious, theatrical, artistic and canny. 'You'll go far', she told me, 'I can spot them, you know! I recognised Tommy Steel long before he became famous'. If anyone should have been a theatrical impresario, it was Monica. She was perfect for launching me as a lecturer and for obtaining the bookings needed to fund expeditions. So great was her faith that she worked feverishly on my behalf for two years without earning a penny; subsidising telephone, stationery and postage costs.

As lecturing became increasingly important, there arose a need to learn to throw my voice and lose distinct characteristics of a Leicester accent, so it was elocution lessons at Miss Olivia Haslar's Speech and Drama School. 'Mr Garratt', she would boom with her overdeveloped timbre, 'deliver Mark Antony's speech to the Romans'. Any hint of languidness would evoke an inevitable 'No, no, no, Mr Garratt, you are speaking to thousands in the open air, speak from the diaphragm. "Friends, Romans, countrymen . . ." come along, Mr Garratt'. Twenty minutes of this was exhausting, whereupon she would change to lessons in clear articulated enunciation. 'Pick a peck of pepper, Mr Garratt – No, no, clip the words, not pick-apeck-of-pepper. Pick a peck of pepper, Mr Garratt'. This rough handling did much for my confidence and enabled me to be heard clearly in the largest halls.

The early months of 1970 were devoted to the book. Entitled *Symphony in Steam*, it was published on 19 October of that year, one of the first colour books to appear on steam. Its immediate success brought a first taste of publicity, including a television appearance, and Blandfords agreed to contract the first two volumes of a projected twelve-volume series called *The Last Steam Locomotives of the World*; a career was formulating from the dream.

Now I could afford a secondhand single lens reflex camera, one which had excellent synchronisation possibilities for night photography. But the choice of a Praktica Nova was to set in motion a miraculous chain of events. Having purchased the camera, I needed technical information on how to use it. Unable to afford long-distance phone calls, I waited until my next visit to London, and from St Pancras Station rang CZ Scientific Instruments, the distributor of Praktica cameras and was put through to Bill Breasley. 'What do you photograph at night?' Bill asked. 'Steam locomotives', I said. 'There aren't any!' he replied. 'No, not here, all over the world', I explained, 'I'm documenting the last steam locomotives of the world'. 'What do you do with the pictures?' he asked. 'I write books and give lectures'. Then he said, 'Would you consider lecturing for us?' Never will I forget hearing those words; there was a pause and my heart began to pound as I blurted out a grateful acceptance.

So began a ten-year relationship with Praktica during which the company paid a supporting fee for each lecture I gave in return for publicising the use of Pentacon equipment. To have obtained backing from Britain's leading camera distributor was a chance in a million, and the most single important factor in surviving those incredibly difficult years. Praktica also suggested an approach to Agfa, whose colour film I used exclusively. Jimmy Bake, Agfa's Press and Public Relations Officer was fascinated by my quest to cover the world. Over a tray of tea served amid the inspiring Victorian portals of Leicester's Grand Hotel, Jimmy agreed that, in return for publicity on the lecture platform and in publications, Agfa would help with film for the expeditions, thus beginning a working relationship which continues to this day.

To launch the series, Volume 1 required a spectacular cover picture. There was no need to look far, as Leicester Power Station had an immaculate red-liveried Robert Stephenson & Hawthorn 0-4-0 saddle tank locomotive, and I dreamed of her flinging a pall of fire into the night sky, against the silhouetted power-station chimneys. The vision haunted me until, dressed in my best clothes, I visited Gordon Caddy, the station superintendent, and offered him the opportunity to have his engine on the front cover. How could he refuse? His response hardly matched my enthusiasm, 'You'll have to pay for the coal', he said dourly, 'about £5 – and for a driver to come in on overtime'. It came to more than a week's income, but their co-operation enabled the mental image become a reality, and one of my best pictures was made.

As work increased, life in the bedsit became even more difficult; it was noisy and costs were rising. Then, in 1971, the third Judy exerted her influence. Judy Hampton was still at school when I met her, but with the blessing of her family invited me to stay at their home in a quiet part of the city. As an only child I had never known a large family, but there now began several blissfully happy years during which I was protected from economic reality and even allowed to use the family car for lectures if it was impossible to travel by train. The vehicle was soon in need of replacement, largely because I had vastly increased the mileage, but instead of part-exchanging it, Judy's father, Dr Hampton, gave it to me. If success could not be achieved from such a series of lucky breaks, it never would, and improved economic circumstances now enabled several expeditions to be initiated. Finances still forbade any long-haul tours, but trips into Europe with a tent were feasible and, in the summer of 1972, I undertook a three-month expedition to France, Italy and Yugoslavia, accompanied on the first half by Judy Hampton, and on the second by Judy Warner.

There was little left in France other than 141R class 2-8-2s, more than 1,300 of which were supplied by North American builders after the ravages of World War II. The 141Rs were confined to the Mediterranean coastline, hauling freight, between Narbonne and the Spanish border and, having covered the

1,600km journey, we located our tent next to a stone viaduct at Rivesaltes. It proved an early lesson in patience, as only several 141Rs passed daily and timings were irregular, so I had to sit for hours at a time, camera at the ready. But the task was urgent as these Mikados were ending a 150-year-long tradition of steam traction on French Railways.

Italy retained a varied fleet of old locomotives, whose origins dated back to the standardisation plan of 1905 when the country's railways were nationalised. By far the most important were the Franco-Crostis, an Italian concept which represented a gallant attempt to improve the steam locomotive's low thermal efficiency by passing the hot gases through two pre-heater drums slung on either side of the engine's boiler. The drums contained feedwater and thus the maximum degree of calorific value was wrung from the gases.

Italy's Franco-Crostis were one of the most interesting locomotive designs in the world and, as only a few survived, it was imperative that good pictures were obtained. Unfortunately they were working in Northern Italy, amid a flat and featureless landscape, 'The Cabbage Patch', as we called it. The approach of midsummer meant a high sun and hard light for much of the day, which left the wheels in inky shadow whilst the engines were filthy black with not a hint of colour. Seldom were there any visible effects, as the steam evaporated the second it left the chimney, whilst the coal used gave a little smoke. Added to these difficulties were the sparse services and if a good location was found for low-angle sun, the chances were that no train would pass. After three weeks of chasing along dreary secondary lines, we moved on, having achieved little photographically, and I determined to return to Italy at a time of year when the light would be more favourable.

Yugoslavia's locomotive heritage was one of the richest on earth as a result of political carve-ups during two world wars. One priority was the 38 class Liberations built in Lancashire for the United Nations by Vulcan Foundry after World War II. The survivors were operating a secondary line deep in Croatia, and once again we made our base next to a scenic viaduct that carried the line over a river. The ideal photographic point was from a rock in the middle of the river, and I was innocently perched there one afternoon when a shepherd with some sheep appeared on the river bank. There was something strangely sinister about him and hesitancy set in when he beckoned me towards him. As I approached, he reached out to take the camera from around my neck; a menacing stare pressed the point. Then I noticed his shoes; too expensive for a shepherd. Up on the hillside another figure stood next to a black car. There was no choice but to hand over the camera and follow my captors. We were driven a long way through remote hilly country not knowing who these men were until, to our relief, we stopped outside a police HQ. Now we could explain; but no one spoke a word of English. Desperately I drew a steam locomotive on the chief's blotter and then pointed to the camera. Everyone looked unimpressed.

'The one that got away'. I didn't know it at the time but this was to be my only picture of a Franco Crosti.

After some hours an English-speaking waiter was contacted in a town forty-eight kilometres away, but it was almost midnight before he arrived. The chief looked deeply unhappy. 'Everyone knows what a steam engine looks like,' he carped, 'why photograph it?' 'Please', begged the waiter, 'they do not believe you. What were you really doing there?' Apparently they suspected that we were working for the Croat Nationalists, by photographing the bridge in preparation for setting incendiary devices. Our vehicle and luggage was searched and after a sleepless night we were driven to the border with Slovenia and instructed never to enter Croatia again.

Realising that we would encounter constant trouble in Yugoslavia, we motored to Belgrade and spent two long weeks struggling to get some form of permit to undertake photography. Eventually permission was won to visit the depot at Novi Sad. As requested, I read out the types known to be allocated there and these were carefully printed on the permit. Having promised not to include the shed buildings in any pictures, we commenced photography under the watchful eye of an officious guide, who became disturbed when he noticed one class of engine in the yard not specified on the paper. Determined that not even its buffer should appear in any picture, he became hysterical when I put a long focus lens on the camera. Assuming this to be super wide angle, he obdurately stood in front of the camera. In sheer panic the depot foreman telephoned the police and, while I was arguing with the guide that the lens showed less and not more, a Volkswagen van with its blue light flashing swooped into the yard in a cloud of dust, and twelve uniformed policemen jumped out. Under the direction of the foreman, the offending engine, an innocent 0-6-0 shunting tank of Serbian origin, was driven safely out of range. Once gone, the policemen piled back into the van and with blue light still flashing, roared away in true Keystone Cops fashion.

Fortunately conditions were more reasonable in the old Austrian territory of Slovenia, and the expedition ended successfully. Sufficient material had been obtained to release Volume 2, *Masterpieces in Steam*, but I determined to undertake one more expedition before releasing the book, and where better than Finland during the Arctic winter with its blizzards and snowy landscape? So, in January 1973, I set off with Judy Hampton for a six-week trip that would take us over the Arctic Circle into Finnish Lapland.

Our principal objective in Finland was to depict the trains amid driving blizzards and we were lucky to arrange an eight-hour footplate journey from Rovaniemi northwards over the Arctic Circle. Our locomotive was TR 1 2-8-2 No 1074 and we were due away at 2.41am. A swirling snowstorm was sweeping across Rovaniemi when the lights of our engine came into view, hauling a string of empty ballast wagons bound for the Rajavi Quarries sixty-four kilometres into Lapland, from which we would return with a gravel train.

Chilled, and covered in snow, we mounted No 1074's footplate to find a cheery crew who seemed pleased, if a little surprised, that English visitors should be joining them. Upon drawing out of the yard we entered a world of extremes, as from the hot roaring locomotive one looked out into the Arctic blizzards sweeping across the desolate white landscape. Silent, green conifer trees slid past endlessly, lit to a momentary brilliance by the cab's flickering orange glow. The huge engine charged northwards like some anguished giant on the rampage; seldom before had steam engines appeared so exciting.

After an hour the driver shut off steam, seemingly in the middle of nowhere and, waving a powerful hand torch, he beckoned us over to his window and shone his light out into the snowy blackness. Minutes later he found his target as the torch's beam illuminated the Arctic Circle sign; we had entered Lapland. It is moments such as this which dispel language difficulties, man communicating freely with man.

Speed soon returned to the engine's permitted maximum of 88km/h and I took a turn at firing, noticing that the logs and coal on the tender were completely white with snow; looking ahead, the Mikado's blazing headlamps showed the single track to be completely snowed over; ours was the first train over this lonely route for some hours and we gained the eerie sensation that we were no longer running on rails.

During our wait at Rajavi, Malno, our fireman, demonstrated his way of making coffee by filling an ancient blackened kettle with water, hooking it onto the end of a firepricker and extending it into the firebox. After boiling point was reached, it was drawn out and ten teaspoonfuls of ground coffee were added, whereupon it was left to stew along with a couple of huge Finnish skinned sausages on the Friedman injector mount. Never did food taste so good as in that remote Lapland quarry.

Dawn broke as we returned towards Rovaniemi and Lapland's beauty impressed itself upon me. Reindeer tracks could be seen alongside the railway, whilst the grip of winter rendered the innumerable lakes and rivers invisible, their presence being indicated by a lack of trees. With a deep throaty roar No 1074 sped its heavy train southwards, flushing pairs of willow grouse from the lineside bushes and leaving inky black smoke trails across the sky. At 8am we rolled into Rovaniemi and the Arctic venture came to a close. The snowy scenes we had photographed provided a marvellous contrast to the sunny European pictures and the soot-laden themes of British industrials.

The material for *Masterpieces* was released, whilst *Twilight*, which had been published in 1972, was sufficiently successful for Blandfords to issue a contract for Volume 3, *Africa*, so heralding the first long-haul expedition, scheduled for the summer of 1973. All available funds had to be mustered to finance this tour; bank and building society accounts were closed and I left the country accompanied by Judy Warner, without a penny to my name. But the dream to document the world's last steam locomotives was beginning to materialise.

·4·
Africa – the First Major Expedition

The humid, scented night was alive with the sound of insects; it was the primeval Africa of storybooks. We were in the Gabon, having touched down for refuelling on our flight to Johannesburg. But any illusion of an archetypal dark continent waiting to be explored vanished upon arrival, as the modernity of South Africa was characterised by frosty mornings unfolding into endless days of iridescent blue skies.

Our first introduction to South Africa's railways was the busy line between Pretoria and Witbank, worked by the 15C type 4-8-2s built by Baldwin & Alco during the 1920s. In common with many South African lines, this route undulated like a sheet of corrugated iron. How the 15Cs pounded over it! Their harsh staccato exhausts were audible from afar as they charged furiously up the banks with a sharp spitting beat, like the sound of a stick striking a tightly stretched snaredrum. Upon reaching the summit they would fall silent and coast down the other side.

On the nearby Witbank Coalfield many old British locomotives were active. A prime location was the Transvaal Navigation Colliery where former Rhodesian Railway's 16 class 2-8-2+2-8-2 Garratt No 609 worked the long connection from the colliery to the main line. The 16s were first exported by Beyer Peacock in 1929 and were superficially similar to the LMS Garratts of the same period. How wonderful to hear the syncopated roar of a Garratt once again, a sound I hadn't heard since 1958 when the last LMS examples disappeared from the Midland main line.

South Africa's most dramatic steam operations were on the north–south main line running from the Cape, through South Africa, and on into Rhodesia. This route formed a significant part of Cecil Rhodes' dream of a railway from the Cape to Cairo. Leaving the Transvaal, Judy and I drove several hundred kilometres south to begin work on this line, starting with the Kroonstad to Bloemfontein section, widely regarded at the time as the world's busiest steam-worked route. One hundred trains, many double-headed, passed over this 186km section every day. Services were dominated by the 15F and 23 class 4-8-2s of the 1930s. How these engines dashed across the winter veldt with driving wheels spinning in a shimmering tapestry of movement! Dust trails swirled up alongside their enormous rakes and the engines' chime whistles

Witbank shed . . . maybe you can smell the soot, smell the oil, and so glean something of the incredible atmosphere of these last cathedrals of steam.

resounded far over the flat lands. Exactly how hard these engines worked was indicated by cinders lying 30cm thick, often as much as 12m from the line sides. When steaming hard, the 4-8-2s consumed 100 gallons of water per kilometre, and each month the fire-raking and watering point at Vetrivier provided the locomotives with 68 million litres of water whilst 1,400 tons of ash was shovelled from the pits.

Further south the main line traversed the arid Great Karroo Desert, where the mighty condensing 4-8-4s were active. From De Aar the condensers worked through the desert to Beaufort West. Northbound operations were handled by their sisters, the 25 class non-condensers which were employed on the busy all-steam section to Kimberley. De Aar was like a dream come true; the smell, bridled pressure and sheer power of giant engines towering around us, brought back memories of twenty years previously; it could have been Crewe North.

The sense of pride pre-eminent at De Aar reflected the best of nineteenth-century railway traditions. Engines were spotless, from the humblest shunter upwards, and the crews were forbidden to slip the engines or emit heavy smoke. A policy of one man, one engine, was instituted on the 25 NCs and many were named after the drivers' wives; apparently some men thought more of their locomotives than their wives. Crews vied fiercely for pride of place; cab interiors were immaculate, bedecked with burnished brass embellishments.

Judy and I spent a week photographing the condensers, following them from De Aar into the wild Karroo; a treeless and stunted expanse, home of the aardvark, the rock dassie, cape raven and pied crow. Sunny days, inky nights, and purple twilight dramas all passed uninterrupted except for the swelling rolls of locomotive smoke hanging between the hills like a storm cloud.

Further south in Port Elizabeth was a location for a classic theme which took several days to complete. It was the study of a Pacific crossing an embankment at speed with an eleven-coach train. The setting was superb, all that was needed was a magnificent pall of black smoke echoing the train's length. To achieve this Judy was placed on a station one and a half kilometres down the line to brief the crew to make smoke when passing the camera point. On the first day the train passed magnificently, but the smoke was insufficient for the drama I sought. We repeated the theme on the second day, and the crew made a better effort, but still not enough for my satisfaction. On the third afternoon, Judy repeated the request. The crew were incredulous, 'We have done it for two days', they insisted. 'But my friend needs more', Judy explained. 'Can you do better?' Fortunately they entered into the spirit and decided to give this ridiculous Englishman what he wanted. The train approached with such a spectacular exhaust trail that I could hardly hold the camera still for excitement. The resulting picture, called 'Port Elizabeth Express', has appeared in many books and is undeniably one of my finest.

We renewed our acquaintance with Garratt engines in Natal, having driven north-eastwards from Port Elizabeth through the Transkei. The target was Masons Mill depot in Pietermaritzburg. Here the mighty GMA 4-8-2+2-8-4s built in Britain and Germany during the 1950s were employed on tortuously difficult lines up to Franklin and Greytown. Masons Mill had the largest allocation of Garratts in the world; eighty-nine locomotives, with not a conventional engine in sight! The GMAs were ferocious masses of seething energy and to witness these grotesque restless engines looming out from the gloom of their vast depot was intensely moving.

Having covered our priorities in South Africa we began the long drive to Bulawayo in Rhodesia where the Garratts reign supreme. We were now in British territory – albeit under the Smith regime – and resistance was encountered when asking for photographic permits.

Frustrated, and anticipating hours of fruitless debate and inaction, Judy and I went to the Railway Security Headquarters to be greeted by a burly Yorkshireman complete with broad accent, 'I'm sorry', said the chief, 'thear's still noa word 'bout yer papers'. Apparently, government officials had concluded

Our smoky triumph at Port Elizabeth, after three days of waiting the picture was made in 1/500th second.

that I was a railway expert deployed by the British Government to identify the origin of sanction-breaking diesels. Incredulous, having come halfway round the world to see a steam fleet, knowing and caring little for diesels, I remonstrated long and hard until it was decided that we could continue our task on the condition we reported regularly to the head of Regional Security. 'That wey, nowt's in writing', said the chief.

At last the programme could begin and we spent our first week on the Bulawayo to West Nicholson line. This route is worked by the 14A Class 2-6-2+2-6-2 Garratts exported from Beyer Peacock's Gorton Works in 1953. The line is typically African in its remoteness, traversing undulating rocky terrain sparsely animated with stunted bush. Twists, curves, gradients, culverts and lonely wayside crossings; definitive Garratt country. The best photographic location for a 14A was crossing one of the larger river bridges so we intercepted a train and asked the crew to make a big smoke as they passed the spot. Returning to prepare for the picture, we met a track ganger. 'Don't go into that riverbed', he said, 'the place is alive with crocodiles. Several are old and will attack'. But the 14As were an important Rhodesian type and the sky was decked with superb mottled clouds, making the perfect backdrop. 'We've got to risk it!' I told Judy. Precariously making our way into the riverbed, we set up a position amongst the reeds. Had a crocodile approached from the direction of the bridge we would have been cut off, as our only retreat was through swamp. A whole hour passed but no train; several times we heard disturbances in the reeds and froze with fear. The clouds that promised to be our ally were thickening, and periods of sunshine becoming less.

Just as we heard the 14A's whistle, a mass of cloud drifted over the sun. 'We've lost the picture,' I said in anguish. We heard the train approaching, but it didn't seem to be getting nearer. This mystified us until we realised that the crew, having seen the cloud, had stopped the train and were poised to charge across the bridge with a great smoke trail the second the sun came out again. And that is exactly what happened; the instant the sun burst out the Garratt's regulator was opened and she stormed across the viaduct in epic style, emitting a glorious, brown smoke trail in her wake. We fired the shutters and our shouts of joy were mixed with the terror of being pounced upon by a crocodile as we fled to the safety of the embankment.

Satisfied with the picture made of the 14A Garratt, we began the long journey westwards across Rhodesia to Wankie, a vibrant coal-rail community close to the Zambian border. From here a quarter of a million tons of coal each month were transported along the main line to Bulawayo by Manchester-built Garratts. We could have been in the heart of the Ruhr; barking locomotives, the smell of sulphur, and flaming coke ovens; whilst not five kilometres away elephants, giraffes, lions and leopards could be easily sighted in the surrounding bush.

We stayed at the Old Wankie Hotel, and each night a class 12 4-8-2 came up from nearby Thompson Junction to shunt the works. We would watch her from the hotel's verandah. Vomiting flames, she strove towards the yards, with flaming droplets of incandescent fuel bouncing along beneath until in a frenzied cacophony she slipped. Friction sparks flew from the rails, to be promptly doused by orange-tinted jets of steam from the sanding apparatus. The struggle continued as flaming cinders were flung skywards with incredible velocity. Like an ejaculating Roman candle, the old-timer found her feet and dug into the rails with renewed vigour. The engine's progress could be followed as she shunted, and each time the fireman added a round of coal, a copper-shrouded inferno danced in the swirling smoke trails. The old class 12 belonged to Rhodesian Railways and was one of a large class of 4-8-2s built by North British during the 1920s.

After spending a week in this remarkable environment photographing the 12s along with the huge 20 class Garratts which take the coal hauls from Wankie to Bulawayo, our work in Rhodesia was completed and we returned to Johannesburg. Shortage of funds now forced Judy to return to England leaving me to complete the final month in East Africa alone.

The main attraction of East Africa was the 530km-long line from Mombasa on the Indian Ocean, to the Kenyan capital, Nairobi. This metre-gauge line was host to the largest steam locomotives left on earth, the majestic 250 ton 4-8-2+ 2-8-4 Mountain class Garratts built by Beyer Peacock in 1955, and named by the British after the highest mountains of East Africa. During that incredible journey, the trains climbed the equivalent of 1.5km in altitude, Nairobi being situated on a 1,524m plateau. The journey time with a 1,200 tonne freight train was twenty-two hours.

Some British officials remained on the East African Railways, and I was befriended in Nairobi by Graham and Mary Hoare, who helped with photographic papers and a car in which to travel down to Mombasa. I made a base at Voi, one of several oil and water stops, and stayed at the Voi Game Lodge in the heart of the Tsavo Reserve, noted for its elephants and marauding, man-eating lions. A few miles north of the lodge it was possible to see the world's largest steam engines taking water alongside the world's largest animals, for at Tsavo River the Mountain engines take water on an embankment above a river where elephants come to drink. The Garratts were decked in gorgeous maroon livery, and their names – *Menengai Crater, Uluguru Mountains* and *Ol Donya Sabuk* – evoked grandeur befitting the locomotives perfectly.

After days with the Mountains, I would return to the game lodge, and watch the sun drench the hills with a counterpane of light and shadow as the twilight slowly advanced. Hawks circling above brought a gentle momentum to the evening stillness, whilst in the valley below a whistle rang out to herald a red Garratt snaking its long silver box freight across the valley floor. A red backing on her nameplate indicated that it was *Mount Kilimanjaro*. There are times, I thought, when Kenya comes close to the tourist brochure claim of being 'God's Own Paradise'.

I came down to earth with a bump in Mombasa when my car was broken into, and all the photographic equipment stolen. Here was I on a prime location, thousands of miles from home, and no photographic equipment! Fortunately all exposed films – apart from those in the camera – were safely back at the hotel. I returned to Graham and Mary and asked whether they could help to obtain sufficient equipment to complete the expedition. Eventually an Asian photographic dealer lent me cameras on trust.

'The Cattle Boy' sits on the bank of a Ganges tributary as this Indian version of the Flying Scotsman *rumbles over the arches.*

Wild poppies invigorate a turn of the century Mallet as she threads through the East German countryside with an early morning train from Gernrode to Alexisbad.

Overleaf:
The unforgettable sunsets of the Nile. Classic British semaphores and signalbox at Khartoum.

Graham and Mary were worried by my determination to drive to Tabora in Tanzania. 'The journey is through wild scrub terrain', Graham said, 'you need a Land-Rover and a companion for such a trip'. But I had been delayed enough and was determined to reach Tabora as soon as possible. Goaded by images of red British engines in this remote outpost, I left Nairobi and headed out along dust roads into wild scrubland. I was terrified. I had been foolish to undertake the journey alone; the road degenerated into a cart track and the country was desolate. My vehicle became a raging bronco: stones pounded the underside and an enormous cloud of dust pursued me all the way.

By nightfall I was exhausted and, upon reaching the shanty town of Babati could go no further. It was a place of vegetables, scattering chickens, bustling women and handcarts; my vehicle looked totally out of place. I obtained a room in a decrepit oil-lit boarding house and was offered chicken and rice for supper. Apart from being too tired to eat, I realised that the poor bird would probably have been killed to order and imagined the chef chasing the chicken up the main street!

Next day the landscape grew bleaker. I passed Africans of various tribes, some out hunting with bows and arrows. By noon the hilly country was behind me, and the road descended into a vast plateau of breathtaking beauty. Far across this tableland lay Tabora, served by the railway which ran from the coast at Dar-es-Salaam to Mwanza on Lake Victoria's shores. Twice the vehicle got stuck in dust mounds which lay on the road like snowdrifts, but shortly before midnight, in a state of feverish exhaustion, I reached the Tabora Hotel.

Tabora was one of the last outposts of Tanzanian steam traction, and the smiling array of red engines which peeped from the German-built roundhouse was worth the effort I had made to get there: 2-6-2Ts from Bagnalls of Stafford; British-built 4-8-0s from fifty years ago; and of course, the famous Tribals, built by North British and by the Vulcan Foundry for the railways of East Africa.

The most interesting route from Tabora was the Mpanda line; a 331km journey through arid tangled scrub country, infested with tsetse flies. This line was worked by No 2611, a scruffy, down-at-heel 2-8-2 built in Lancashire, and nicknamed 'The Crate'. Although her British thoroughbred lines were distorted by a Giesel chimney, a Weir feed water heater and by an air-brake cylinder, she was captivating. No 2611 was the last survivor of the Tanganyika Railways ML class and specially retained on account of her 9¾ ton axle loading.

Even here, the last vestiges of British rule were apparent. At the shed the chief fitter was Jim Field from Andover, and later that day I was to meet the operations superintendent, John Cross, whose family came from Northamptonshire. John offered to attach an inspection saloon to the mixed train bound

Flagging Off, a China Railway's JS Class leading a southbound freight, receives the all clear from Sankong yard in Harbin amid a winter temperature of 25C.

Mountain Class Garratt No 5922 Mount Blackett *negotiates the Mazeras Snake as she climbs the steep coastal escarpment from Mombasa. The train's last wagon has just disappeared round the distant bend!*

for Mpanda, a round trip of two and a half days. The following evening all equipment was stowed into the saloon, and I joined the crew on No 2611.

However humble the engine, there is something deeply exhilarating about footplate riding; you belong with the privileged few, high as a pulpit and lofty as a throne. Soon Tabora faded into the arid waste and 2611's anguished roar became the pulse of Africa and sole companion of the now purple twilight. From the footplate of 'The Crate' I viewed the shambled dwellings of African villages. Around large wood fires set in village squares, swarthy bodies swayed rhythmically pounding maize with poles. The fires became less frequent until blackness took command, relieved only by the engine's yellow glow bathing the tracksides like molten steel and revealing hyenas gaping incredulously at man's intrusion of their domain.

But now was the dry season, and all the way up to Mpanda we delivered water to remote tribes. Upon arrival we shunted the lonely yard and collected four wagons of wheat, a sugar van and some empty water tanks before returning. At dusk we reached Ugalla River, an infamous crocodile- and hippo-infested region. With wheel flanges screeching, 'The Crate' eased her train over the rickety track, which was built on a boulder embankment protruding above the water line. There was a raging sunset, and our train must have looked gold-plated to fishermen watching from their tiny wooden boats.

Back in Tabora yard, I collected my belongings from the saloon, and as I did so No 2611 trundled past on her way to the shed. A flurry of steam, a whistle, a wave, and she was gone. The tour had come to an end.

Memories of the long journey back to Nairobi, through the Serengeti National Park, will remain for ever. On the second day a torrential deluge turned the dirt road into a raging river. The vehicle got bogged down with its rear axle beneath the mud. Had I been alone the situation would have been desperate, but fortunately I was accompanied by Leif Gobal, a Swede, and expert navigator. The two of us managed to eventually free the vehicle by placing branches under the back wheels. We worked feverishly through the deluge but it was almost midnight before we were on the road again.

The Serengeti's Game Protection Law permits travel by daylight only, and all vehicles must be booked into lodges by dusk. Sure enough the animals came out in force, the track frequently being blocked by herds of zebra, rhino, elephant, giraffe, wildebeeste and buffalo, which loomed in our vehicle's lights amid the total darkness all around. Inching up did not move them, and we had to nudge them with the front bumper, whereupon the herd suddenly took flight. Instead of dashing off in all directions, they thundered along the track ahead of us, and we followed them over long distances.

We reached the lodge mudstained and exhausted, but as I fell into bed that night I felt only exhilaration; the first major expedition had been successful beyond my wildest dreams.

·5·
Iron Dinosaurs

The suburban train rattled its way out of Victoria. I viewed my fellow passengers dispassionately; most were lost within their *Evening Standards* and crosswords. It was an hour to East Grinstead and my mind wandered over the pictures made in South Africa. The engines had been functional and 'normal' in appearance. Somehow a contrast was required for the next book. The antiquated and bizarre on remote tropical lines? South East Asia, I mused; engines with shades of Rowland Emett? Images of huge iron dinosaurs. Yes, that's it! *Iron Dinosaurs* would be the title for Volume 4. By the time we reached East Grinstead the concept was firmly established; I mentioned it to the secretary of the camera club who met me at the station, 'Sounds fine', he replied. Four months later the expedition was under way.

I left the Hamptons, not before time, as Judy had got engaged to somebody else. My worldly possessions were dumped in Monica's garage and every penny was invested in the expedition. On 9 July 1974 I set off for Java, Sumatra and the Philippines, to be joined by Judy Warner three weeks later.

The Indonesian State Railways had 900 steam locomotives on its books, embracing 70 different classes, some of nineteenth-century origin, and many having come from builders whose names had long since become a revered part of railway history. So antiquated were the country's railways that the islands were regarded as a 'Galapagos' of steam. After a night in Jakarta, I took a morning flight to Medan, the capital of neighbouring Sumatra.

My taxi from the airport was an old American car of Prohibition period styling, that would have looked battered on a stock car circuit. The doors were illfitting, the windows were jammed, seats were split with stuffing missing, the roof was buckled and there was a gaping hole in the floor through which the exhaust could be seen trailing along the ground. Flanking the streets were dwellings ranging from modern tiled houses with ornately shuttered windows, to crude thatch huts. Corrugated iron walls hugged the litter-ridden banks of the tepid, evil-smelling river; whilst homeless individuals lived without sanitation under market stalls, bridges and even beneath vehicles undergoing repairs in roadside yards. American pop music of the 1950s howled out from cafes and street bazaars through cracked amplification systems. It was to this environment that I had to respond.

A base was made at Siantar deep within the palm oil plantations where nutshell-burning 0-4-4-0T or Mallets of Dutch origin were active. Also in the area were turn-of-the-century 0-4-4Ts with a hint of Johnson Midland styling, some 2-4-4Ts – a most unusual wheel arrangement – along with a batch of very handsome Dutch 2-6-4 suburban tanks introduced by Werkspoor of Amsterdam during World War I.

From Siantar I made a trip, by the 'Siantar Express' bus, to a remarkable quarry line at Gunung Kataren. The bus, all colours of the rainbow and characterised by broken windows and a marked lack of usable seats, arrived with horn blaring to clear some errant chickens – the property of people in the queue. The crowd swarmed over the vehicle, cycles and sacks of rice were hauled on top, baggage was roped to the sides, whilst the two doors quickly swallowed up both chickens and crowd. I ended up sitting on the commodious lap of a large Indonesian lady with hens at my feet and a large sack of grain pressing against my left ear.

We set off at breakneck speed – whoever named it the Siantar Express wasn't joking! During the fifty-minute journey, the horn blew furiously as the bus was aimed along narrow, congested roads; I could hardly believe my ears when piped music began to gaily rollick from a speaker not twenty-five centimetres above my head. But for all the discomfort, I was amongst friends – although few could do more than wink and say, 'Hellow mister'. Dutifully they set me down in the middle of a dense forest, having pointed to a footpath through the trees. A resounding cheer went up as the bus moved away with a sea of smiling faces peering from every window. I was well into the forest before the combined sounds of music and the bus's screaming engine finally died away.

It was midmorning and the heat was debilitating. Soaked in sweat I emerged from the trees to be confronted by a primitive stonecrusher, the purpose of the railway being to carry stones up from a riverbed to a connection with the Indonesian State Railway system, for use as track ballast. Alongside the crusher stood engine No 106, an 0-6-0T from Ducroo & Brauns of Weesp, Holland. Raising my camera to assess the composition, the viewfinder brushed against my left eye and by a strange quirk my contact lens slipped out and fell into the jungle at my feet. A wave of nausea passed over me; those lenses were vital for photography, no funds having been available to bring a spare set. I stared at the thick jungle realising the hopelessness of my dilemma; no substitute would be available in Indonesia; the tour would be a failure.

I remained riveted to the spot in sheer desperation, and eventually attracted the attention of the workmen at the stonecrusher. They moved to within a short distance from me and stood staring with stark expressions. Pathetically I pointed to my eye and then into the jungle: how could they know what a contact lens was in this remote Sumatran outpost? Yet, their faces showed comprehension and, encouraged, I pointed to the nail of my little finger to indicate the size, and again to my eye and back to the jungle. They conversed amongst themselves and calling several colleagues ten of the men formed a circle around me. Each man went down on his haunches and began to dissect the jungle, leaf by leaf.

After an hour I was standing in the middle of a circle of bare earth about a metre in diameter. Suddenly, one of the men gave a shout and, rising shakily to his feet, held on the tip of his extended finger the missing lens; everyone cheered and shouted, their tongues incommunicable.

I loved the Indonesian people and was happy to be amongst them, but a readiness to trust caused one nasty incident. One evening when walking back to the hotel, I was called across to a small drinking bar. Not wanting to appear unsociable I went over, and entered a wooden shack to be confronted by a rough-looking man with an enormous belly. Around him were several murderous-looking characters. A glass of fearsome local spirit called *raki* was pushed in front of me. The big man swayed on his chair and, pointing to the glass, bellowed, 'Drink with Pappy'. Politely declining the offer stirred Pappy into a drunken rage, and he began to shout abuse. His henchmen then tried to make me drink. A firmer refusal caused Pappy to lambaste his men for not making the Englishman drink and events took an alarming turn when amidst the affray I noticed one character brandishing a vicious-looking knife. In his temper, Pappy upset a bottle of spirit, and as he lunged across the table to catch the rolling bottle, attentions were momentarily diverted. Blessed with superhuman energy, I made a desperate lunge for the door and fled for my life, to the tune of Pappy's insane bellowing and the heavy sound of drunken brigands attempting pursuit. The calm, ordered atmosphere of the hotel was an ascendancy to heaven.

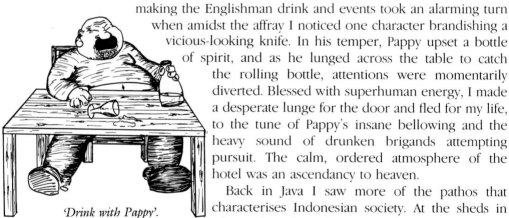

'Drink with Pappy'.

Back in Java I saw more of the pathos that characterises Indonesian society. At the sheds in Jakarta, the cabs and empty tender areas of derelict engines were used as dwellings, complete with fitted curtains and linoleum floors, whilst lines of washing added colourful valances to the driving wheels of several engines. I remember peering into the open smokebox door of a derelict Krupp D52 class 2-8-2 to find a mother suckling a young baby.

Among Java's classic types were the B51 4-4-0s, which had a distinct Prussian ancestry. Forty of these two-cylinder compound express passenger engines were delivered to the then Dutch East Indies between 1900 and 1909, principally by the German builders Hanomag and Hartmann. I was told that they worked from the outskirts of Jakarta up to Rangkasbitung, but after two days waiting in Jakarta none was seen; I decided to travel by diesel-hauled train up to

Rangkasbitung at six o'clock on the third morning, but upon arriving at the station found the coaches jammed with people. Assuming the engine to be a better place to undertake the long journey in excessive heat, I made my way up to the front; no relief there, either! There were seventy-five people on that loco-motive, a modest 3ft 6in-gauge secondary line diesel; twenty-three were in the cab and the remainder situated on the front, sides and top; undaunted I was hauled aboard. The driver was wedged into the corner of his cab, from which he could see nothing of the track ahead; an agreement existed with the horde on the roof, that should an emergency arise, they would bang on the engine's sides! The only passengers who paid were those travelling inside the compart-ments; the engine was the driver's preserve – no ticket collectors infiltrated that domain. Any compassion I felt for the driver on this trip was dissipated when the hat came round. The driver's collection was half the price of the normal fare, no tickets issued and no questions asked.

I found a B51 at Rangkasbitung; how she evoked images of her ancestors rolling majestically across the Prussian plains. I climbed into the cab. Boiler pressure was up and the engine was tensely vibrating. After a while the crew arrived and, acknowledging my presence with a smile, they backed the engine onto a rake of decrepit coaches in the station. To my amazement I discovered that the B51's steam brake had been disconnected and our only means of stop-ping was with a dubious-looking handbrake on the tender. At first I had hoped the train might be going to Jakarta, but the engine was facing west. It was my intention to return to Jakarta that night as all my belongings were in the hotel there, but suddenly the engine moved forward; at first I assumed this to be a station movement but within seconds realised that a journey had begun; I was being spirited away.

I had no idea where we were going and communication with the crew was impossible. Any ideas of my getting off at the first station were banished, as the likelihood of even returning to Rangkasbitung that night was remote.

The B51 burned a mixture of coal, wood and oil. A pungent, frothy smoke swept continually around the cab and down the train. The B51 was opened up and like an anguished beast headed ferociously through the darkening land-scape, violently lurching over the rough track bends. Heading through the darkness we could have been hitting 160km/h. With many kilometres behind us the country began to flatten out and we passed over rice paddies, above which fireflies danced amid the brilliantly cascading flurry of sparks coming from the engine.

After two hours the lights of a distant town became visible – our destination had been reached; we were in Labuan on Java's west coast. The engine was to remain there overnight, returning to Rangkasbitung at 5am the following morning. The crew, realising my predicament, ordered a *betjak* to lead me to accommodation. I bade them goodnight, promising to rejoin them the next morning. A call was arranged for me at 4.15am but the combination of over-exhaustion and belligerent mosquitoes throughout the night banished any hope of real sleep, and then it wasn't until after 5am that the call came. I dashed through the empty streets towards the station, hoping that the train might still be there, but when I heard the familiar exhaust beat and whistle call, I knew that the B51 was on her way. Now, caught out for a second time, I dismally watched the sun rise to herald another day of intense heat.

The next train was not due until afternoon, assuming it ran at all, and I was persuaded to catch a bus direct to Jakarta. It was a harrowing, hair-raising journey, the sum total of minor incidents en route being: two punctures; overheated engine; loss of entire cargo of rice from roof; and a dangerous skid which promised to terminate in a stagnant pond. Fatalities were three squashed chickens and possibly a dog that leapt out of the bus into thick undergrowth. It would be an economy in effort if Indonesian bus drivers were to leave their hooters on and switch them off when not needed. I arrived in Jakarta in a state of nervous exhaustion seven hours after leaving Labuan.

It was now time to meet Judy at Jakarta airport before the expedition continued into central Java where an exotic mix of locomotives awaited us. The active list included 2-8-8-0 four-cylinder compound Mallets in the volcanic highlands, handsome lean Pacifics from Werkspoor of Amsterdam, German-built 2-6-0Ts from the 1880s and some of the world's last 0-4-0 tram engines.

In Jogjakarta we found an incredible dump which included four 0-4-2 tender engines with large-diameter coupled wheels. They were almost certainly the last surviving standard gauge 0-4-2 passenger engines in the world and though reduced to a blaze of rust and obscured by heavy vegetation, their classic British styling was unmistakable. They had been exported by Beyer Peacock during the 1880s but their design was older as they bore a generic resemblance to Beyer Peacock's *Ilfracombe Goods* of 1873. They hadn't turned a wheel in thirty years; certainly not since the Japanese invaded Java in 1942 and shipped away all standard gauge equipment to Manchuria. Amongst the 0-4-2s was an outside-framed 0-6-0 goods engine of 1885, also from Beyer Peacock; this gem was similar to the Kirtleys built for the Midland Railway between 1863–74.

The highlight on Java, however, was the B50 class 2-4-0s built at Sharp Stewart's Great Bridgewater Street Works in Manchester during the early 1880s. They survived on the lightly laid branch from Madiun to Ponorogo, hauling trains comprised of three four-wheeled coaches that lacked doors, lights, luggage racks and seats!

The 2-4-0, like the 0-4-2, was one of the earliest forms of passenger engine, and riding footplate on the B50 was like a journey into locomotive history. Their ailing condition, combined with the appalling state of the track, forbade anything better than a crawl, and the thirty-two-kilometre journey took three hours – an average speed of 10.66km/h!

Having spent two months in Indonesia, we continued to Hong Kong to process our films at Agfa's laboratory before proceeding to Manila, capital of the Philippines. From here an internal flight took us to Bacolod City on Negros, an island crisscrossed with sugar plantation railways that were host to a fine variety of 3ft 6in-gauge American motive power ranging from Moguls to 0-6-0 saddle tanks.

Also on Negros was a legendary logging railway operated by the Insular Lumber Company. This system had vertical-cylinder Shays and an 0-6-6-0 four-cylinder compound Mallet built by Baldwin of Philadelphia in 1925. This Mallet had fascinated me for years; she was the ultimate iron dinosaur and running her to earth was the fulfilment of a long dream.

Having made our base at the Sea-Breeze Hotel in Bacolod, we decided to tackle Insular Lumber first. Its operations centred upon Fabrica in the north; the journey took several hours on wet, crowded roads and it was almost dark when we arrived. Upon reporting to Insular's operations office, I was told that the general manager had gone up to base camp, at Minapasuk, and would not return until the next day. I asked about the Mallet, and Conrado Gabrielle, the operations superintendent, said 'You mean No 7; she is on her way down from Minapasuk with a loaded train and will be here in about three hours'.

Fascinated by our mission, Conrado took us to a nearby shanty-type coffee stall where local coffee, boiling in a tub, was strained through sacking before being poured into table glasses. 'No 7 is a strange one', Conrado said, shaking his head, 'she's a mankiller. More people have died through that engine than I care to mention – some say she is haunted.'

Eventually the phone rang in the control office and Conrado dashed across the road and, standing outlined against the light streaming through the doorway, called, 'No 7 is within three kilometres'. Shortly afterwards a whistle rang out in the damp atmosphere and resounded through the hillsides like a cold shiver. Minutes later the crossing-gates over the Bacolod–Sagay road rattled down, and the big mahogany-burning Mallet appeared, running tender first.

She was twice as large as I had imagined; a freakish conglomeration of locomotion. The crossing lights revealed a faded green livery, although her ornate eight-wheeled tender was black with white lettering which proclaimed INSULAR LUMBER CO – 'no riders allowed'. She was the weirdest engine I had ever seen, but it was a tantalising glimpse; she had gone within seconds, her huge log cars piled high with mahogany trunks rumbled after her into the gloom.

Next day Conrado arranged with the general manager, Simplicio Moreno, for us to stay in his house at Minapasuk. This would enable us to see the loading operation and, apart from capturing my dream picture of a Shay and the Mallet side by side at the dead of night bathed in fire, would also enable us to depict No 7 crossing the famous American trestle viaduct at Himog-An.

No sooner had we arrived at Minapasuk than a typhoon burst over neighbouring islands and heavy dark clouds brought torrential rain that lasted three days. During that storm the track disappeared beneath a sea of mud, yet the indomitable Shays unstintingly went about their duties and continued whirring their way along at full throttle, maintaining the usual 160km/h.

The only time at which the night picture could be made was when Lima-built Shay No 12 took the logs to the exchange siding as No 7 arrived with the empties. Then, for a few moments, the two engines would be side by side. On several nights we were alerted that the Mallet had left Fabrica with empties, but she invariably derailed on the way, the track being in a terrible state of repair, and she didn't reach Minapasuk until after dawn.

On the sixth evening, shortly before midnight, we received a call to Moreno's house saying that the Mallet was on her way. We gave her three hours before assembling the flash units and setting off for the exchange siding. 'We may be lucky tonight', Moreno said as we trudged through the wet jungle.

The sidings were deathly quiet; only the gentle simmering of the Shay was audible. I felt very nervous and began to doubt that we would ever get the picture; dawn would break within the hour. Then, to my surging joy, a familiar whistle rang out through the distant groves accompanied by a weird syncopated offbeat roar as the four cylinders, all out of alignment, could be heard working above a cacophony of steam leaks. Ten minutes later the terrifying Mallet drew up alongside. In the halflight, bathed in fire, she looked like some hideous creature from Hell. 'Keep away from her', Moreno said, 'she's dangerous, concentrate on your photography'. The Shay sprang to life and the two antiquities stood side by side, fire swirling from their chimneys. The session was so exciting that I could hardly operate the camera and control the lighting units. But when dawn broke I had succeeded in putting onto film one of the last classic American-styled logging railways left in the world, and one that ended the great traditions of the American Pacific North West.

The cane-cutting season was just beginning on Negros and, at Ma Ao Sugar Central south of Bacolod, the manager and his wife, Guillermo and Dorothy Araneta, welcomed us cordially and we were invited to stay at their palatial home, which had a colonial atmosphere – spacious and comfortable with a large domestic staff keen to ensure maximum comfort and offer exotic cuisine.

Guillermo was a gentle, pensive man with an intellectual air, and he took us down to the factory's locomotive sheds. The motley array of dead engines that greeted us looked like the contents of a scrapyard. 'Don't worry', Guillermo said, 'they will all be working in a few days' time when we start milling'. He was abashed at the state of the fleet, but I assured him how wonderful they were. 'We've come halfway round the world to see such blissful decrepitude as this', I said. Most of the engines were hybridised but all of pure American extraction; 'Don't ever paint them', I begged Guillermo, 'you are running one of the most amazing steam fleets in the world'. He laughed but didn't really understand.

Many adventures at Ma Ao took place during the nightshift, and we would book a regular call at midnight and take the 2am haul along the Cutcut line. Apart from providing an opportunity to do night photography this line ended at the base of a huge volcano and was particularly photogenic. Ma Ao's No 5 – a Mogul built by the American Locomotive Company in 1924 – was the most decrepit engine of all; she often worked this turn and, running tender first, would propel a huge line of empty wagons out into the darkened fields. Usually Judy and I sat up on the back of the tender as the footplate was extremely cramped with driver and two firemen working strenuously. Two firemen were essential with these engines as they burn bagasse, the natural waste product of sugar cane processing. This fuel costs nothing, but is low in calorific value, and when the engines are working hard a mass of the strawlike substance is lifted from the fire bed, drawn through the tubes and flung, still burning, from the chimney. And as we climbed towards the volcano the fire effects from our engine were quite spectacular.

When dawn broke activity began along the line. Water buffaloes hauled cart-loads of cane to the railheads, whilst the migrant labourers loaded it into the

The haunted Mallet No 7 with Shay No 12 spraying the tropical vegetation with fire during our epic night session at Minapasuk.

A Carabao makes a timely arrival at the railhead with a load of sugar cane as an American Mogul from the twenties draws in with empty wagons from Ma Ao Sugar Central.

wagons. The sun would be up by the time we reached the end of the line and, looking back over the billowing oceans of sugar cane, we could just discern the chimneys of Ma Ao factory some thirty-two kilometres distant.

One day as we began our descent from the volcano, No 5 was running chimney first, with fifteen loaded wagons in tow. We resumed our position on the tender top and were busily gnawing away at succulent sticks of sugar cane when I noticed that the last four wagons had become separated from the train, and were trailing some way behind us. We were beginning to climb a short gradient and the breakaway, having occurred at the top of an incline, meant that the wagons were likely to catch us up and hit us with force. I knew from talking to the crews that this was a common happening and some very nasty accidents have come about in this way, as upon striking the train, the wagons would frequently rear into the air.

There was no doubt, the wagons *were* catching up! Screaming to the driver produced little effect, so flinging myself onto the fuel and tumbling through it towards the cab, I renewed my shouts, whereupon the driver, sensing rather than hearing, realised that something was wrong. Noticing the runaways, he accelerated No 5, with full regulator and achieved sufficient speed to equal that of the wagons and all we felt was a gentle bump as they hit us. Inspection proved that one of the pins which attaches the couplings had snapped in half. This was replaced from a reserve supply on the locomotive and we continued our journey.

Operations were so exciting at Ma Ao that we went out during the afternoons as well, often up to the coastal wharf at Pulupandan with five thirty-ton vans of soft brown sugar. We would return to the factory in time for a late dinner and then, after a couple of hours' rest, would travel with the 2am working on the Cutcut line. We did this for three consecutive days during which we didn't sleep a wink but did achieve the most wonderful variety of pictures. One theme, however, which I had set my heart on, had not yet been secured – an exotic sunset with the amazing No 5.

On the third morning the Cutcut train arrived back at midday and we reached the Aranetas' too tired to eat. The day had been cloudy, but just before we were about to fall into bed I noticed the clouds breaking up, heralding a raging sunset – the type that has made the Philippines famous all over the world. 'Look', I said to Judy with some trepidation, 'there will be a sunset tonight'. I can see now her look of excited anguish. 'You want to stay up?' she said. 'Can you?' I asked. Despite our exhaustion, we both knew the answer; the sky was already breaking up into massive lumps of cumulus cloud and the sun beginning to dip. 'Go on,' Judy said, 'ring the control office and see if we can take an engine out at 6'. I rang through to the traffic controller's office and connected with our friend, Agapito Corpez. 'I thought you had gone to bed', he said incredulously, 'you haven't slept for three days!' 'Never mind that, we need an engine for tonight's sunset', I said. 'Can you provide us with an engine for two hours this evening from six to eight o'clock?' 'How about No 5?' Agapito replied, 'she won't be going out until two o'clock on the Cutcut diagram'. We kept awake that afternoon with burning anticipation of a classic picture. Having drunk several mugs of black coffee, we set off with our equipment and reached the shed to find No 5 standing ready in the yard, whereupon we ran light engine out into the fields, as the sun slowly went down in a raging red ball. After several miles the perfect place was found and we stopped in a loop to wait for the sunset. As we had an hour to spare, we got the lighting units up and the camera in position, whereupon a picnic was spread out on the grass beside our locomotive and we enjoyed a traditional Philippine meal of shrimps, rice, chicken and shellfish, followed by locally grown fruits and coffee. Exhaustion was now forgotten as we became wildly excited by the sunset. It could not have been better had we orchestrated it ourselves, as, backed by a violent orange glow, the broken clouds reflected a myriad of different colours. With bated breath we waited for its beauty to mature until deep twilight set in with the sky still a mass of excitement against which No 5 sat simmering, curling wisps of bagasse into the air with a flickering reflection of her fire in the cab. The flash units exploded one by one to our shouts of elation. This session promised to produce a materpiece. No 5 was incredible enough on her own, but against one of the world's most celebrated sunsets she pushed photography to the sublime.

·6·
Hard Times

100 HOURS A WEEK, 52 WEEKS A YEAR

Penniless and homeless I returned to Britain. The greyness of that November in 1974 was relieved only by memories of the expedition and brilliant pictures made. The photographs were my greatest asset.

The only money I had was £100 in travellers cheques from the tour. It was a bleak outlook; where to go from here? One saving grace was that Monica had a good season of lecture bookings, and although most were small clubs offering low fees, they might, with luck, sustain me through the winter.

In an attempt to achieve some stability, I presented myself on the doorstep of an old flame. Her parents agreed to let me stay, but Stephanie, feeling compromised, had me thrown out within three days. There was no alternative but to move into an hotel in nearby Kibworth Beauchamp. It was comfortable, but my odd working hours made it difficult to appear for breakfast before the nine o'clock deadline. Indignant that even ten minutes' lateness deprived me of a full breakfast, I complained to the owner. On my third night there, I returned at 1am from a lecture to find that my stay had been terminated. With the owner's steely gaze penetrating the rear of my vehicle, I drove out of the grounds and headed for Leicester.

It was starting to snow and, realising that I couldn't sleep in the car, I determined to find a room. Only the biggest hotels had someone on duty, and the three that I tried were all full. It was 3.30am when I reached the Holiday Inn. Past caring about the price, I took a sumptuous room at £45 a night, expensive in 1974 by most people's standards, but half of my total estate! For the sheer hell of it I decided to go the whole hog and ate a full English breakfast the next morning, whilst considering my next move. The money was down to £15, so another night at the Holiday Inn was impossible. That day I combed the city in search of a boarding house, eventually taking a room overlooking the main London Road.

I reflected gloomily on the events of the past forty-eight hours. I was 34, and penniless in a cheap boarding house. It was a frightening mess financially; ten days in the boarding house consumed my lecture fees as fast as they were earned. A feeling of dejection with the inevitable overtones of failure set in.

At the eleventh hour I was rescued by Judy Warner's mother, who invited me to stay at her bungalow until somewhere permanent could be found. One evening, shortly before Christmas, she said there was a cottage available for rent at Newton Harcourt, 'your old trainspotting village'. The steam trains may have gone, yet thoughts of the countryside around Newton remained as beautiful and comforting as ever. But the idea was untenable; I could never afford to rent a cottage, let alone furnish it! 'It is furnished', she retorted tartly, 'and you should go and see it!'

Next day, we drove to Newton Harcourt, and to our amazement we found that the cottage overlooked the very bridge from which I had watched that first train in 1949. Even the old water pump where I had assuaged my thirst as a boy stood derelict in the square. The rent for this romantic country abode? Eight pounds a week, and although the commitment was frightening, refusal was impossible. On 1 January 1975, I moved in. Actually, living in Newton Harcourt was a great psychological advantage; I had come full circle, and happy associations provided a stability long since forgotten. But my childhood paradise of rambling hedges, copses, gurgling brooks, wild flowers, birds and animals, were all in the process of being destroyed. Familiar meadows were becoming chemically polluted prairies, and much of the surrounding country-side was becoming as barren and decimated as the railway itself. Yet as the wind blew through the village square that winter it bore the ghostly rhythms of a Jubilee tackling the southward climb, laced with the call of barn owls, skylarks and partridges.

The difficulties of keeping on an even keel financially were legion. Despite returning from lectures in the early hours, I needed to be in the study by nine o'clock in order to write the manuscripts and articles vital for supplementing my income. Any progress made was immediately engulfed by inflation, then rampant. A minimum 100-hour week was the harsh reality of economic survival. Had I dropped to a six-day week, or had reduced my working hours, I would have gone under. It was touch and go. The awful sluggishness of my economy – six years after turning professional – was debilitating. The work necessitated abandoning all social activities, relationships and interests. This was acceptable; but to helplessly watch the heritage diminish at an ever-increasing rate – whole railway networks vanishing into oblivion – before I could reach them, was a constant source of anger and frustration. Then Blandford announced that the projected twelve-volume series on the *Last Steam Locomotives of the World* was not commercially viable! They would contract Volume 5, but only if it were confined to Europe. This series had been a guiding ideal and vital source of funding and its abandonment came as a devastating blow.

Throughout this period I was fortified by Monica's insistence that we would 'make it'. Resigning myself to years of dedicated toil before circumstances improved, I prayed my strength would hold out. The die was cast; there was no turning back; I would eat crusts if necessary.

Plans were made for the European expedition to begin in April, after the lecture season had ended. Two weeks before the departure date I was busy with preparations when the phone rang. It was Stephanie. She didn't admit it, but it was evident that she wanted to renew the relationship. All reasonable instincts to leave well alone, including Monica's infallible intuition, were ignored. Dreams and preoccupations of years past could not be cast aside. An inner compulsion drove me to cancel the expedition. Within three months Stephanie and I were married and had set up at the cottage in Newton Harcourt.

That traumatic summer of 1975 provided time to consolidate resources; the financial knife-edge with which the year had begun, had by Christmas eased slightly. Contracts for other books were coming in and I was in increasing demand as a lecturer. The European expedition had still to be fulfilled, and these better circumstances enabled me to buy an old Commer motor caravan with which to do the tour. The book was to be called *Veterans In Steam*, and when the lecture season finished at the end of March, Stephanie and I set off on a five-month expedition that would embrace East Germany, Austria, Italy, Greece, Turkey and down through Syria to the border with Jordan and the Lebanon. Another piece of the jigsaw had fallen into place.

We were happy; the bleak circumstances of the previous year were dispelling and the future looked brighter. Little did I realise the devastating effect my lifestyle was to exact upon our marriage.

The cottage at Newton Harcourt

·7·
Overland to the Middle East

There can be few better tests for a new marriage than five months of living in a tiny motor caravan. Having left Newton Harcourt, Stephanie and I headed across Europe, bound for East Germany where the last high-speed steam expresses were ending their days in a blaze of glory.

Most Communist countries are hazardous for the photographer, but East Germany is a happy exception, although restrictions did force us to stay on official campsites. Our base was at Moritzburg, just a few miles from the main line, to the north of Dresden.

The expresses were worked by the fabulous 0-1 Pacifics of 1925. Though half a century old, these thoroughbreds were hauling trains of 500 tons in weight on scheduled timings faster than a mile a minute – nearly 100km/h – with top speeds of 144km/h. On our first evening, we drove over to the main line to watch the 17.03 out of Dresden climb the bank through Weinböhla. Running like a well-oiled sewing machine, the Pacific confidently swept through the wooded countryside and throbbed up the bank with nothing more than a heat-haze rising from the chimney; her huge red driving wheels, 6ft 6¾in in diameter, spinning gloriously. Flocks of linnets rose from lineside bushes as the express swept northwards, and wafts of oily sulphur drifted across the banks. It was wonderful that such scintillating performances could be experienced in Europe as late as 1976. The busy service also included a number of heavy international expresses, such as Bratislava-to-Berlin with Czechoslovakian coaches or Sophia-to-Berlin with Bulgarian, Hungarian and Czechoslovakian stock. If one took into consideration the East German coaches along with the red dining cars, up to five different liveries could be seen on one train, thus providing a truly international flavour.

The last steam expresses constituted a milestone in railway history, and we stayed for three weeks before moving south to Italy to try again with the Franco-Crostis. By this time only two survived, working between Cremona and Pavia. Although light conditions were better, the dreary environment reasserted itself. But we persevered; there would not be another chance. After a month's arduous pursuit, we finally achieved some worthwhile pictures, partly due to the marvellous spirit of the train crews who got so used to seeing the Commer parked up on the roadway ahead of location, that a sighting resulted in automatic black smoke.

Before leaving for Greece it seemed sensible to check that the Crosti films were satisfactory, as the engine's withdrawal was imminent. The films were sent to a laboratory in Milan for urgent processing. This occasioned one of the greatest tragedies of my career. A strike at the plant had caused chaos and the pictures were returned ruined; the grain structure had broken up and every image was characterised by a greenish-blue cast. After weeks of toil we were left with nothing. But saddest of all was the discovery upon returning to Cremona that the two Crostis were withdrawn the very day our films were processed! We had lost the pictures of one of the most fascinating steam survivors on earth. Since then, all films have been returned to the complete reliability of Agfa's plant in Wimbledon, to prevent such a disaster from ever happening again.

The journey to Greece necessitated passing through Yugoslavia, and negotiating the infamous Belgrade Highway, part of the international trucking route between Europe, Asia and the Middle East. From Zagreb to Belgrade was 400km (two hundred and fifty miles) of sheer horror with burnt-out wrecks every few kilometres. All along the route small crosses decked with wreaths stood on the roadsides, and often included photographs of the victims peering out through the encroaching blades of grass.

Greece had already said farewell to the steam age, but our visit was to be one of a succession of pilgrimages made to her historic graveyards. Apart from their photographic allure, the dumps contained a number of rare and significant locomotives. Several sites lay around the country, both on the standard-gauge system in the north and the metre-gauge system on the Peloponnisos peninsula. Our journey through Yugoslavia, brought us conveniently to Thessaloniki, where in two separate dumps we found British WD-type 2-10-0s; American S160 2-8-0s; United States Army Transportation Corps 0-6-0Ts, along with 0-10-0 and 2-10-0 designs which dated back to the days of the Hapsburg Empire.

We continued southwards through the blistering heat of the Greek summer, in search of the metre-gauge dumps on Peloponnisos. In Athens we learnt that a graveyard existed somewhere in the mountains between Corinth and Tripolis; we headed into the wild boulder-strewn beauty of Peloponnisos and received directions in Tripolis.

We located the place, but having driven to the nearest point along the floor of a valley, there was nothing to be seen. We surveyed the railway as it wound its way round the hills and crossed the valley on a huge viaduct. But there was positively no dump. We returned to Tripolis to take new bearings, only to be given the same information.

'The Wreck of Tithorea'. One stormy night this hapless engine crashed in the hills on the main line between Athens and Thessalonika. She was pushed into a coppice and forgotten. I visited the lonely hulk many times to record her ghostly moods.

The insistence of Greek officials persuaded me to try again. We returned to the valley; the rubble tracks petered out before the viaduct and I left Stephanie with the Commer and set off along the valley floor on foot. It was a distance of about a kilometre and the track bed could be seen clearly on both hillsides. Within a hundred metres of the viaduct, I noticed that the line originally hugged the mountainside to the head of the valley, whereupon it had come back down the other side. The viaduct simply replaced the dog's-leg. As this revelation dawned I caught sight of an engine, and there, perched high up on the mountainside, stood a long line of rusted metre-gauge locomotives, standing on the old track and entirely camouflaged in the rocky terrain.

The dump contained several of the historic McArthur 2-8-2s of World War II design, along with a number of the old French-built Z class 2-6-0Ts, which in their antiquity resembled the type of locomotive painted by Monet in his Saint Lazare series.

These necropolises are irresistible; the abundance of wild flowers provides an evocative foil to the corroding hulks, whilst the rusty tonalities on the engines offer a subtle range of colours which would be the envy of any artist's palette.

The days we spent in the Peloponnisos graveyards, amid the peace and tranquillity of the olive groves, were a welcome break before the long journey towards Turkey. We had no permits to work in Turkey, as the months of letter writing to various ministries in Ankara had produced no reply. But determined to grasp the nettle, we drove straight to the Aegean port of Izmir, traditionally famous for its figs, but now for its suburban steam workings.

The great train-watching place in Izmir was a signal box known as Poste B, where the routes from Alsancak and Basmane stations crossed. Here we were privileged to see such delights as former Prussian G8/G10 0-8-0s, 0-10-0s respectively; German-built 2-10-2s of the 1930s; German (war engine) 2-10-0s; French-built 2-8-0s from Humboldt of Paris; along with some racy-looking British 2-8-2s from Robert Stephenson's of Darlington. After passing Poste B, the Alsancak line climbs sharply through teeming suburbs and curves upwards against a stunning backdrop of mosques, minarets and houses, perched upon every conceivable inch of a vast hillside.

This location was a photographer's paradise, and Stephanie and I journeyed eagerly along the line to begin taking pictures. Almost immediately we became aware of two sinister-looking individuals in plain clothes, watching us intently. They could have been innocent bystanders fascinated by foreigners with cameras, but I suspected something worse; their presence was likely to lead to an arrest. We watched a few evening suburban trains come up the bank, making the most magnificent exhaust, but I had no will to photograph them, feeling naked without a paper of authority. Meanwhile the figures continued to gaze in our direction.

But Turkey was to prove a bittersweet mixture, for in the midst of this dilemma a couple came down the hillside and invited us into their home. They were so persuasive that we acquiesced, and minutes later were surrounded by their family – eight in all. Our hosts were determined to prepare a meal in our honour. It is Turkish custom to sit in a circle on the floor and eat communally from an enormous bowl. When this arrived, my worst fears were realised. It was the classic Turkish dish of sheep's intestines and yoghurt! In the midst of this predicament, I turned to look from the house windows to see the two plain-clothes individuals carefully inspecting the Commer. I wished that they would come and arrest us on the spot! When we finally managed to escape the family's hospitality, the two sinister figures watched impassively from a rocky defile on the adjacent hillside. This incident convinced us that some papers were essential. Determined not to waste any more time, we undertook the 640km journey to Ankara overnight in order to obtain them.

We discovered that any authority to photograph railway installations must bear the signatures of all chiefs of the armed services, the Ministry of Foreign Affairs, the State Police, and, of course, the Railway Ministry. Even with good-will such a task would be formidable. We felt tired and downcast. Turkey was one of the most important countries in the world for my task. Here we were, in the capital with obstructions bedevilling every move we made.

Dejectedly we returned to the Commer and began to cook breakfast on the Railway Ministry car park, discussing what to do. Then, out of the blue, a hand-some young Turk appeared, who spoke perfect English. He was Rifat Köksal, his father was an opposition Member of Parliament, and he promised to obtain the necessary papers for us. Meanwhile, we were installed in a luxury flat in the Chankaya district of Ankara, where we lived like VIPs. We dined at the exclusive Anatolian Club normally attended only by members of the Government and Senate; we visited a sitting of the Senate itself and socialised with generals and government ministers alike. They were fascinated with the work that we had come to do, but unbelievably none of them could obtain a simple piece of paper enabling us to photograph obsolete steam locomotives. For two weeks, Rifat devoted all his energies to our needs; he was a loyal Turk and wanted to show his country in a good light.

But by the beginning of the third week, Rifat had to admit that our papers would take 'more time'. He suggested that we proceed to Syria and return after a month, by which time the papers would be ready. With Rifat and his father involved, we could not risk working without papers as it could reflect adversely on the very people who had tried to help us. So we loaded the Commer and set off due south from Ankara, bound for the Syrian border.

Our journey across the vast Anatolian Plain as we headed towards the Taurus Mountains revealed more incredulous aspects of the country.

Every few miles gangs of ghoulish youths with shaved heads and an uncanny resemblance to Genghis Khan, would appear at the roadside waiting for foreign vehicles. One of the youths would then hold up a packet of cigarettes, whilst behind him stood several of his friends with boulders in their hands. We quickly got the point; either foreigners threw out 'smokes' to the youths or they pelted the vehicle. They meant it, too! The first groups we encountered received nothing more than a 'thumbs-up' as we sped by, whereupon a huge boulder hit the Commer's roof with an almighty bang.

Once into Syria, the landscape became ever more golden and the temperature seemed to soar with every mile. 'At last', I said to Stephanie, 'we will get back to the railway'; it had been a month since we had done any photography. Steam was supposed to be thriving in Aleppo, but we were three weeks too late! All standard-gauge locomotives had been withdrawn and the entire fleet dumped at Jebrim, seventeen kilometres away.

Our only hope now was the narrow-gauge system based around Damascus, from which two routes radiate; one over the mountains to Beirut in the Lebanon, whilst the other is the northern end of the Hijaz, through which passes the famous Pilgrim Route to Mecca, authorised by the Sultan of Turkey during the Ottoman period.

The pilgrim route to Mecca. We often rode footplate between Damascus and Der'a on the Jordanian border, and here our train has stopped in the middle of the desert to allow an Arab farmer to get down.

Fears that steam may also have finished in Damascus were dispelled upon visiting the systems shed and works in Cadem. Here steam was abundant in gloriously vintage form. The line to the Lebanon was worked by some delightful Swiss-built 2-6-0Ts and 0-6-2Ts, along with several 0-4-4-2T Mallets; whilst the old Pilgrim Route was operated by 2-8-0s and Mikados from Hartmann of Chemnitz. Also present were several 2-8-0s from Borsig; these were particularly handsome locomotives and a fine example of their builder's 'English' phase of design. Seven different classes were noted in Cadem's shed; all built between 1894 and 1918.

Although we had official papers permitting photography in Syria, the language barrier posed insuperable difficulties. Then came another lucky break; we met Hamid El How, who not only knew English, but insisted that we stay at his small farm amid the fertile lands of Dayarra on the outskirts of Damascus.

Dayarra is a famous fruit- and crop-growing area in Syria, a beautiful green oasis irrigated by countless pumps which draw water from underground lakes formed during winter rains. By this method, plums, grapes, peaches, apricots and apples, along with many crops and vegetables thrive. We lived from natural foods around us and bathed in the irrigators. Black desert nights had tremendous beauty, swirls of hot desert air were invigorating, and all of us slept outdoors, under a sky adorned with Van Goghlike stars and lulled to sleep by the chattering of irrigation pumps.

From this base we were able to watch the Swiss tanks working up to Sergayah on the line to Beirut taking city residents for a day in the cool mountains, the heat of the city during high summer being intolerable. Most trains were packed to capacity and had a festive air; people clung to the sides and even sat on the roof. Songs burst from the coaches and mingled with the engines' barking exhausts as they fought their way through a wonderland of yellow rock, glistening under a cobalt blue sky. At Sergayah the engines turned and prepared for the return journey down to Damascus. Paradoxically lines of wagons bound for Beirut stood in the sidings waiting for the Lebanese tragedy to end. It was strange to enjoy the tranquillity of Sergayah and realise that only a few kilometres beyond the mountains a terrible war was being enacted.

After two happy weeks with Hamid and his family we continued south to Der'a, on the border with Syria and Jordan, and an important junction on the Pilgrim Route. Here, a short branch led to Bozra, whilst another line left westwards towards Haifa in Israel. The Bozra line was worked by one of the Borsig 2-8-0s, and I told the depot foreman of our wish to photograph her. Next evening he intimated that she would be in the shed yard at ten o'clock. 'Take your chance now', he said, 'she's going on the Haifa line with a tomato special tomorrow'. The engine was large and black and needed eight different flash heads for enough light. These attracted attention from passers-by, and a small group formed to watch our activities. It was midnight before we returned to the Commer, delighted with the pictures we had achieved.

During the early hours a heavy pounding sounded on the Commer's door. Opening up we were confronted by six men. 'Police', one of them snapped, 'hand over the films you have taken tonight'. Nervously I presented our papers of authority, but they were thrust back unread. Suddenly the dreadful truth dawned; a convoy of tanks had passed by as we were photographing the Borsig and someone had assumed we were filming military movements, in what was a sensitive border area. Forced to drive to Damascus amidst a posse of police cars, Stephanie and I were subsequently incarcerated in a grotty underground cell, and our vehicle impounded!

Convinced that we had contravened military security, demands for the film continued. I had hoped that once in Damascus our purpose could be explained. But nothing would persuade our captors of our innocence. The situation became desperate; a decision had to be made. I asked to be taken to the Commer and opened up the safe built into the chassis and removed a spare camera containing blank film. It was a vain attempt, yet to our amazement it worked – the film secured our release. Within the hour we were back on the road and making a dash for the Turkish border in case the film was processed and we were re-arrested.

Two days later, and still in one piece, we entered the suburbs of Ankara, certain that by now Rifat would have our authority. We were greeted like long lost friends, but there were no papers! 'Go and do your work', he said. 'Make out as best you can. This is a good country, no harm will befall you'. Bidding him farewell we set off for Irmak, a village lying to the east of Ankara, on the main line northwards to Zonguldak on the Black Sea Coast. The Zonguldak line was worked by the American-built Skyliner 2-10-0s, but Irmak had a former LMS Stanier 8F 2-8-0 on pilot duty, a type known in Turkey as The Churchills. She was in original condition apart from Westinghouse brake pumps and the substitution of Stanier's deep-toned whistle for the shrill high-pitched affair applied to Turkish engines in general. When shunting, her exhaust beats were so uniquely Stanier 8F, that I was momentarily carried back to the Leicestershire countryside of my childhood. This ghost of Crewe was a glowing fragment of history.

Proceeding northwards to Zonguldak, we followed a route close to the railway, over dirt roads and through barren hills. Several days of linesiding brought us to the steel town of Karabuk amid the remote mountains of northern Turkey, a site specially chosen for reasons of security. After negotiations with the steelworks' security chief we were admitted into the plant. The motive power fleet was predominantly British; two Hawthorn Leslie 0-6-0STs and a couple of Bagnall 0-8-0Ts having been bought specially for the steelworks' opening in 1937. In later years four identical saddle tanks had come from Robert Stephenson & Hawthorn, along with several other industrials from German builders; in all fourteen engines of five different classes.

The sharp staccato bark of steam trains toiling the heavy grades out of Izmir is as characteristic a sound as the emanations from the mosques summoning the faithful to prayer.

But no one knew if photography was allowed. In sheer frustration we watched the Hawthorn Leslie tanks reversing rakes of crimson ingots from the steel furnace; a German 0-6-0T pulling hopper wagons filled with coke; and a Bagnall 0-8-0T propelling a line of slag ladles.

The result of the negotiations was permission to take just one picture and what better than the Bagnall 0-8-0 tipping molten waste from the foundry, down the slag bank; an industrial drama of a bygone age, which illuminated Karabuk's night sky with a ghastly orange glow.

Realising that it was possible to do photography in Turkey without official papers, we returned to Izmir to begin the work we had so nervously shunned two months earlier. We spent an unforgettable week on the hillsides watching the succession of smoky veterans trailing the 1:40 grades away from the city, with that incredible backdrop of houses to the rear.

These spectacular sights brought our expedition to an end. We had been on tour for five months, and it was time to return to England. Innumerable challenges had been faced throughout that summer, but the one that lay ahead was even more daunting – a major season of lectures.

·8·
Treading the Boards

'I'm doing my best, Guv!' expostulated the taxi driver. 'Well, there's a bonus if I'm in time for the midnight train', I shouted whilst being flung around in the back of the cab.

Invariably I would arrive with only minutes, even seconds, to spare. It was the height of the lecture season and no sooner had a show ended than I had to jump into a waiting car to be whisked at breakneck speed to the nearest station. Many of the journeys made were via London and the last train for Leicester left St Pancras at 5 minutes past midnight, after which there would be a wait until 5am.

Throughout the seventies I travelled to my lectures with just a box of slides, and a few books to sell. I took lecturing very seriously, but inexperience often left me at the mercy of my hosts, who were not always as organised as they might have been. Imagine this: the lights are out, the show has begun, when without warning the doors open with a crash and several latecomers clump in. The clubroom is full and chairs have to be passed in an acrobatic manner over the heads of seated people to an accompaniment of bangs, slithers and 'sssh, shush'. Hardly the setting for an interesting evening, especially when the sequence is repeated several times during the first half hour.

The coffee interval can turn into a menace if the washing-up volunteers are given free rein. I remember one evening when 150 members and guests of a prestigious photographic society heard – above the commentary of the second half – not only a horrendous rattling of crockery, but also how Freda's new baby was allergic to its dusting powder! On another occasion – after a faultless start – my show was moving towards a fine climax and the hall was so quiet you could have heard a pin drop. Suddenly, in an adjacent room, the local WI broke into impassioned strains of 'Jerusalem', accompanied by a strident, out of tune piano, and one wayward soul singing in a weird falsetto voice.

Projection problems were legion. An indolent character fumbling around on the projector and dragging the beat on every slide change would not only completely destroy any continuity in commentary, but invariably send the focussing haywire as well. With problems like these, it doesn't matter how hard a speaker tries, all effect is dissipated. There are eight ways to put a slide into a projector, and I have had them all in one night!

I developed a healthy suspicion of projectionists. Sod's Law states that the most illustrious events produce the worst projectionists, and once at an important literary luncheon in East Anglia, the chairlady introduced me to Mr Hestlebotham 'who had done this job for thirty years'. 'Precisely', I thought bitterly as I surveyed my aide, who was well into his 70s, was bent double and had a pronounced squint. Despite my none-too-subtle suggestions that he might want to sit this particular event out, Mr Hestlebotham could not be dissuaded. I need hardly have worried; he was impeccable, every picture was changed on split second cue, and focussing punctiliously managed with a small pair of binoculars.

Mr Hestlebotham.

Another show stopper was an afternoon lecture that I did at a mental hospital in Bristol. The auditorium was full and the patients seemed well disposed to their afternoon's entertainment. No sooner had the second picture appeared on the screen, when a piercing high-pitched cry came from the darkness of the auditorium. 'It's another engine!' the voice shrieked. Ignoring this I plunged into the third picture. The eerie wail came again, 'It's another engine; I don't like engines!' The voice then degenerated into howls and screams. Unable to cope with this outburst I froze, my nerve began to fail, until two white-coated orderlies gently lifted the wailing offender out of her seat and carried her into the corridor outside, but for at least thirty seconds afterwards her continued wails of, 'It's another engine, I don't like engines!' were clearly audible.

Such misdemeanours pale in comparison with the chairlady of a civic society in Wiltshire who announced my lecture ' "Iron Dinosaurs" (Steam Locomotives of South East Asia)' as 'a recitation upon dinosaurs by the well known naturalist Colin Garratt'. I interrupted her as discreetly as possible and whispered that the show was about steam locomotives, whereupon she turned and audibly corrected me in a highly supercilious way. 'Our programme states dinosaurs and natural history', and the malevolent look in her eye indicated that that was exactly what she expected me to do.

Chairmen themselves often get shows off to a bad start by taking five tedious minutes to introduce someone, who, in their own opening words 'needs no introduction'. One rather florid character, who introduced me to a 200-strong audience at a sports and social club in Lancashire,

FERRANTI LTD. CAMERA CLUB

A Slide Lecture

to be given by Colin Garratt

"Iron Dinosaurs"

THURSDAY
NOVEMBER 6th, 1975, at 8.0 p.m.

ADMISSION 10p. **Pay at the door or by ticket**

A lecture for 10p.

proved that he was long-winded in more than one sense when he audibly farted, sending the front row into hysterics.

Once, booked to lecture to a small camera club in Durham, I was amazed upon reaching the venue to find a vast hall with 400 seats set out. Clearly my expenses would not be a problem here, and so, having driven up from the Midlands, I booked myself into a nearby guest house. When I informed the club secretary he visibly turned pale, 'Oh no', he gasped, 'you can stay with us. Go and get your things from the guest house now, I'll ring my wife, and you can stay with us'. Whereupon he ran out of the hall like a startled rabbit. 'Incredible', I thought, gasping at the palatial hall around me, 'how damn mean can these clubs get?' Meanwhile the chairman arrived and knowing nothing of what had transpired, asked me if I would like to see the projector. Puzzled, I followed him along the hall and up four steps which led behind the curtain onto the stage. Here I found a four-foot-square screen and twelve neatly arranged chairs. The club had eight members and always held meetings on stage whenever the hall was free!

By the mid-seventies I was giving a hundred lectures a season involving thousands of kilometres of travelling, often via London. Day or night, winter or summer, I never failed to be inspired by the majestic portals of St Pancras Station. It was the gateway to home, but more important, it personified the magnificence of the railway age. However weary I was, those portals injected a fresh vitality. During the night journeys I studied the work of many painters. Reading and reflecting on the lives of artists strengthened my photography and although I never had time to pick up a camera during the season I was always a better photographer at the end of it.

Galvanised by treading the boards in clubs and schools for six years, I felt that my performance was reaching a professional standard. Now I had the confidence to try for the bigger lecture circuits, and dreamed of being installed on the books of the country's top lecture agencies. One of these is Foyles, an agency of long and proud tradition which has been run for many years by the redoubtable Kay Whalley. I telephoned her, but Miss Whalley had not heard of me, wasn't interested in steam trains and doubted her clients would be either. In any case she had Alan Pegler who talked about the 'Flying Scotsman' and that was quite enough. The telephone conversation ended with the words, 'Mr Garratt there is nothing further to say'. Deflated, I determined to convince Miss Whalley of my worth. Leicestershire has produced many national personalities, but none more gracious than Lady Isobel Barnet who achieved national recognition on 'What's My Line' during the 1950s. She was an accomplished and popular speaker. A recommendation from her might do the trick. So I telephoned her. 'You're the railway man aren't you', she said, and without hesitation invited me to coffee the following morning. During our chat, I outlined my ambitions as a lecturer, and particularly my desire to be on Foyles' list. 'I will have a word with Kay', she said with confidence, 'ring her next week and you will find everything will be all right'.

When next I spoke to Miss Whalley, she was charm itself. 'Isobel's recommendation is good enough for me', she said. 'Please send me photographs and full details of your life and work. Welcome to our books'.

This success led to acceptance by the other leading lecture agency, Associated Speakers, owned by the comedian Cyril Fletcher. Each year 'Associated' held an annual dinner and conference at the Dorchester Hotel, at which the speakers on their books were invited to meet representatives from clubs and societies across the country. Speakers arrived at 11am and assembled

FOYLES LECTURE AGENCY

Colin Garratt

Colin Garratt has photographed the wood-burning engines of the Arctic Circle, taken dramatic pictures of giant steam engines rampaging through the wild landscape of Africa, and tracked down the individually-styled locomotives eking out their days on the romantic islands of Taiwan, Java and Sumatra. Colin Garratt is a fluent speaker with a pleasing personality and a clear voice that can be heard in the largest hall.

LECTURES:

"The Last Steam Locomotives of the World"

"The Steam Giants of Africa"

"The Iron Dinosaurs" — The Emmett-like trains of the romantic islands of Java and Sumatra in remote mines and quarries, sugar fields and isolated logging lines.

"Painting with a Lens" — How classical painting has influenced photographic studies which are shown alongside works of the French Impressionists, Constable, Turner and other artists.

(All with 2 x 2 in. colour slides)

Wilfred Pickles, O.B.E.

Wilfred Pickles has been well-known as a broadcaster for many years and his first appearance on the West End stage was in *The Gay Dog* at the Piccadilly Theatre in 1952. His films include *Billy Liar* and *The Family Way,* and his books, *Between You and Me, Sometime Never,* and *For Your Delight* — an anthology of poetry. He has recently given a programme of his personal choice of poetry, prose, rhymes and stories in the BBC series, *With Great Pleasure.*

LECTURE:
"The Pleasure's Mine"

The write up in Foyles brochure. Below me was Wilfred Pickles ('Have a go') who I remember so well as a child.

'Steam trains? Oh no; we are ladies you see!'

in the adjacent bar and lounges, where large name tags were affixed to our lapels. At 11.30 the ballroom doors were flung open and hundreds of representatives, each grasping the agency's list of speakers, were let loose amongst the lecturers and personalities on offer, to accost them, assess them, and possibly book them for their forthcoming programmes.

It was one of the most colourful and exciting events I have ever experienced; for the programme secretaries it was a day in London to be enjoyed, and many were dressed with a flamboyance reminiscent of Ascot. As a new boy I flung myself in the path of anyone who would look at me. 'Here is a nice young man', a pair of ladies would say. Peering at my name tag, they would eagerly shuffle through the directory and jab an anticipatory finger on my photograph. 'Oh – steam locomotives', they would say with some disdain. 'Not really, we are ladies you see. What a pity, such a nice looking young man too.' I would protest, 'No, not nut and bolt locomotives, but beautiful pictures of engines like paintings, you'll love them'. But I was typecast and the ladies' gazes were fixed elsewhere. So I would continue to dash hither and thither, like most who had yet to earn their spurs, in order to gain maximum attention.

I attended four of these Dorchester events, until they were sadly phased out due to the continuing decline in the lecturing fashion. Television and video were making the logistics of operating a successful lecture network increasingly difficult, whilst inflation continued to increase travelling and hotel expenses. Without the guarantee of packed halls, a realistic level of remuneration was increasingly hard to find. Gone were the days when six or seven hundred people attended celebrity lectures at literary and scientific societies, Everyman's or literary and philosophicals. It is extremely sad that the great social interaction offered by the lecture platform has been debilitated by the predigested and packaged entertainment of television and video.

Despite obvious success on the club circuit, serious inflation meant that my income was not increasing fast enough to fund the global commitments. Economically clubs were hard hit; attendances dropped as people preferred to stay at home, which in turn made clubs reluctant to increase their subscriptions. Few were prepared to make a cover charge even for their better lecturers. It became obvious that the fees Monica was being forced to ask were no longer obtainable on the traditional circuit, despite the obvious goodwill that existed between myself and hundreds of clubs which had supported me during the 1970s.

At the same time, the economic climate inevitably depressed camera sales, and Praktica made it clear that any increase in revenues had to come from the clubs.

By 1979 I was aware that a whole era was coming to an end. Coupled with economic difficulties, I was tired of the fact that my professionalism should be at the mercy of small, disorganised organisations. Matters came to a head at a

Many long years were to pass before I triumphed with ladies' organisations. Autographing my railway photographer book at Huddersfield Ladies Luncheon Club in 1984. (Huddersfield Examiner)

large public show organised by a camera club in Cheshire. It was a sellout; 250 people and not an empty seat. Having travelled up by train, I was horrified to discover that no projector and screen had been provided. Already half of the audience were in their seats. After an impromptu committee meeting, one member dashed off in his car to find a projector and screen, whilst dismally I watched the hall fill to capacity. Twenty minutes later the screen arrived and an apology was given to the audience for the late start.

There then followed a floorshow that even the Crazy Gang couldn't have matched. Two committee members climbed up onto the stage to erect the screen, but rapidly got into a hopeless tangle, somewhat akin to the famous trick deckchair sketch. Eventually the screen jammed half-open and the men wrestled with it for a few minutes before suddenly, the screen flew shut trapping one of the men's fingers, causing him to leap sideways and the screen to fall on the floor. This amused the audience, who evidently considered they deserved some entertainment after sitting patiently for a quarter of an hour. Meanwhile the projector was set up on a table placed on the hall floor, a couple of metres below. This was far too low for the screen perched up on the stage, so a chair was put on the table, followed by a cardboard box, topped with a shaky pile of books. Just as the projector was in position, the box bent and all the books fell on the floor with a crash. The audience roared. And when the two harassed souls who were assembling the projector began to argue audibly about the best way of setting it up, the audience went wild with delight.

Having assembled the structure once again, all seemed complete, until it was discovered that the test slide covered both the screen and half the stage curtains as well. A new argument broke out about whether to move the screen down to the hall floor, or the projector closer to the stage. The audience continued to demonstrate their approval; the last thing they wanted was a lecture. All I wanted to do was go home.

An hour behind schedule the lights were put out for the show to commence. Hardly had I uttered two sentences before there was a crash, the screen went blank and the picture flew up to the ceiling. As a sickening thud sounded in the middle of the hall, I heard the sound of slides falling everywhere. The man who had switched off the lights had fallen over the projector cable on the way back to his seat. On came the lights and when the audience had finally stopped laughing, the club chairman, seeing the hopelessness of the mess, announced that the bar was open.

Although such disasters were few and far between, I yearned to have better control over my shows; and in addition to needing more funds, I wondered how long Praktica would continue to give support for me to appear in small clubs. The scene was set for a new age about to dawn; an age which would enable me to take railways to people in a way I had never dreamed possible. My salvation was a new communication technology called 'Audio-Visual'.

·9·
Adventures in Latin America

ARGENTINA

Two long lecture seasons finally provided the wherewithal to explore the exotic locomotives scattered across Latin America; they surpassed all expectations, such an amazing mix of steam survivors that it took seven months, incorporating five countries – Argentina, Brazil, Paraguay, Uruguay and Chile – to complete the expedition.

The tour had been difficult to conceive until Stephanie and I were invited to establish a working base at the home of Richard Campbell, an Anglo-Argentinian living in the former railway community of Temperley, a suburb of Buenos Aires. Richard possessed a keen awareness of the role Britain played in the building of Latin America's railways. 'This house', he would say proudly, 'was formerly the home of D. S. Purdom, Chief Mechanical Engineer of the Buenos Aires & Great Southern Railway (BAGS)'. We immediately felt at ease with the Campbells, who were clearly determined to protect us from any adversity.

Richard arranged an appointment for us with Colonel Mastropietro of Argentinian Railways. I was accepted as a visiting historian and promised all necessary facilities. Also we were to be accompanied by one of his assistants, Hector Cusinato. Tall and burly, in a double-breasted jacket, he looked like something from *The Godfather*. Hector spoke no English, but from the outset we found communication easy.

After two days with the Campbells it was time to begin work. The sparkle in Richard's eyes palled as he called his parting words, 'I wish you had come fifteen years ago when we had a real railway! Now it's a wreck.'

We met Hector at Constitution Station, Buenos Aires and he had three tickets for the air-conditioned 'El Atlantico' express to Mar del Plata, 400km to the south. We headed across green pampa which, with the help of British steam locomotives, once made Argentina the world's pantry, with millions of tons of grain and beef being conveyed to Atlantic ports. Lonely figures on horseback tended vast herds of cattle and a wild landscape was enhanced by coots, plovers, egrets, and gulls attracted by the swamps following heavy rains. Along the way, disused engine sheds, lifted sidings and broken water columns bore testimony to Richard's words. The route was in dreadful repair and the El Atlantico was slower than the steam expresses of seventy years before. Twice our coach lurched so violently that we were all lifted bodily from our seats.

Mar del Plata is an Argentinian Bournemouth, complete with pier, golf course and English-style houses. The resort was developed by the railway and attracts many visitors, not least for the huge casino – one of the most famous in Latin America. But the shed was a disappointment; steam was due to finish the following April and the only engines present were three 8A class 2-6-2Ts and No 3975 *Charrua* – one of a class of twenty Beyer Peacock 4-6-0s named after Argentinian birds.

At the shed we met George Woodward, an expatriate born in Liverpool. At 85 he retained his Lancashire accent; spoke like George Formby and looked like Lowry. I indicated that we would like an 8A moved for photography, but the Argentinian foreman was not happy to see us. Gesticulating violently, he shouted that he would move the 8A when the British returned the Falklands. Hector's tact and diplomacy saved the situation, and eventually the foreman forgot his tantrum and moved the engine himself.

One of my priorities had been to see a 12A class, two-cylinder compound 4-6-0, introduced by Beyer Peacock in 1907. But there were none at Mar del Plata, although the foreman said one was at the sub-shed in Maipu. During the journey I noticed how the BAGS had a distinct LNER flavour, especially the Great Central section; signals, signal boxes, stations and shed buildings, were all reminiscent.

A bitter disappointment awaited us at Maipu; the 12A lay deep amid the gloom of the depot, dead and out of service. Hopes now centred on Tandil, where two more priority classes were allocated; the three-cylinder 11C 4-8-0s of 1924 and the lovely 15B 4-8-0s of 1948. But a second blow awaited us; all 11Cs were condemned and only one 15B was in steam. Begrimed and run down, she looked majestic her lineage was of the 1930s and reminiscent of an un-rebuilt Patriot. The depot chief did have a note of cheer. One 11C, the only working survivor, could be found at Olvarria.

We reached Olvarria the next day, and being Sunday the town was quiet. As we followed a cinder path through the sidings, on our way to the shed, I realised we could have been in Barnsley. There, simmering in the yard was our 11C class 4-8-0, No 4222. She was very rundown, and the only three-cylinder 4-8-0 left on earth. A Scottish ghost in the form of an 11B class 2-8-0 flitted around the weedstrewn goods yard on pilot duty. Several active 15Bs were also present – our expedition to the BAGS was in the nick of time.

We established a base in Olvarria, and with full co-operation from the authorities, made several footplate journeys with No 4222. It was wonderful to hear the three-cylinder beat as the rundown workhorse climbed away from the town. During these sessions with the 11C, Hector announced that the station superintendent wished to take us to lunch in a very special restaurant, for a 200 course meal; at least, that was what we thought he said, but presumably there was some quirk of language we didn't understand.

The establishment looked normal enough, but the tables did look rather large. After the wine had been chosen the meal arrived – sixty-five different dishes! According to Hector we were expected to try most of them. I ate as much as possible and was complimenting myself upon having made a good effort when the main course arrived. Three waiters deposited 100 dishes; fish, meat, cheese, pasta- or vegetable-based. 'Bon appétit', Hector prompted as we tried to show indebtedness to the superintendent by finding a little more room for what was, by any standard, a beautiful if incredible banquet. Then sure enough 35 gorgeously varied sweets followed – everything from truffles to trifles. By now my stomach hurt and the enormous amount of wine I had drunk to help me sample a respectable number of dishes meant that I was inebriated. There was a 15B leaving with a freight at 4pm and, although I staggered down to the yard, I felt so sluggish that I could do no more than watch it pass.

During that unforgettable lunch we had arranged with the superintendent to travel footplate the next morning on a 15B which was taking a freight to Las Flores. The train was booked to leave Olvarria at 8.20.

We left on time with engine No 1576. Her design was definitively British, in which could be seen many other types, as apart from the un-rebuilt Patriots already mentioned, I saw LMS Crabs, SR Lord Nelson and L & Y Dreadnoughts.

Soon we were galloping across the Pampa tableland, heading for the pretty town of Las Flores. Our train must have looked lovely to the distant rancheros riding on horseback, our long line of wagons silhouetted against huge storm clouds into which our engine sent palls of swirling white steam.

'Eccentrico Hombre' at Azul.

Upon reaching Azul, our engine had shunting to do and Hector took us to the station for coffee, where I was approached by a travelling showman dressed in a huge black sombrero and red shawl. His white teeth flashed beneath his Mississippi gambler's moustache as he opened cases containing whips, knives, books of poetry – and several packs of pornographic sketches. I was fascinated but Hector – possibly through feelings of national pride – was clearly embarrassed and, drawing me away, dismissed the showman as 'eccentrico'. As we drank our coffee my anger boiled up over the decrepit state of the railway; the grimy, spluttering diesel-electrics had done nothing to transform the BAGS other than increase its deficits. I thought of the great days of the BAGS, and the pride displayed by its employees. To see Argentina desecrated by road hauliers' petty profiteering made me sick; a once proud railway reduced to nothing more than an overmanned joke. Every time I sounded off in this way, Hector would helplessly shrug his shoulders in agreement and say, 'lunicato'. He was a true railwayman and though patient and co-operative at all times, I sensed that he never really understood my motives as a photographer.

Throughout our travels I had been looking for a BE 0-6-0 saddle tank; a standard shunting type introduced by North British in 1904 for Argentina's 5ft 6in-gauge lines. If there was a survivor, it would be one of the world's last examples of this definitive form of engine. By sheer good fortune we got confirmation that one was working at Bahia Blanca on the Atlantic Coast. My adrenalin began to flow; nearby was the huge naval base at Puerto Belgrano and I had long suspected that old British main line types were working there, drawing supplies from incoming ships. Mention of the base caused Hector to baulk, 'Private and prohibited', he said grimly, 'no aliens allowed – impossible'. But I bided my time, and on the train journey to Bahia Blanca raised the subject again by asking Hector if he could ascertain what type of engine was working at the base. Though he was clearly uneasy, there was, by this time, a sufficient bond between us and he agreed to try.

The depot for Bahia Blanca is Ingeniero White, and sure enough our BE was there. She was gorgeous; a typical British saddle tank with a nineteenth-century aura, not dissimilar in shape to the famous Caley Pugs. I was reminded of how the private builders used to 'peep over the wall' to see what the main line companies' works were doing before designing their products. Sadly she was filthy and could not represent her dynasty in this condition, so I requested permission to paint her. Hector finally realised the truth of the words 'mad dogs and Englishmen'. Ignoring his disbelief, I dragged him to town to get two tins of red paint. Stephanie cleaned off the buffer beam, running plate and

What a glorious sight that high stepping Edwardian beauty made as she backed out of the high security naval base. Notice how her huge wheels dwarf the driver as he applies a round of oil.

coupling rods before liberally applying the paint colour; 'Ultimo historico', I said in my ever blossoming Spanish to the astounded group watching.

It was cloudy during the painting but no sooner had we finished than the sun filtered through the blackened windows to throw lovely mottles over the veteran tank. The bright colour, rippling sunlight and constantly darting shadows were like an Impressionist painting come to life. The pictures were superb.

Meanwhile Hector had been making enquiries about the naval base and came back with a piece of paper on which was written 'Beyer Peacock 1907'. My imagination soared; surely they couldn't have a 12A express engine! I begged Hector to get more information; he told me I was a 'fanatico'. But he did agree to stay at Bahia Blanca until the matter had been resolved.

Contact was made with the naval authorities for a visit, but the answer was a firm 'no'. Hector mimed that he would be shot if he tried to get us in, and was all set for us to return to Buenos Aires, until I had a brainwave. 'Hector, if they won't let us in to see the engine, would they let the engine out to us?' I asked excitedly. By now nothing surprised him and he promised to see what he could do. Finally the answer came – 'Yes – for the ridiculous Englishman who has come halfway round the world after a locomotive – we will oblige!' Arrangements were made for the engine to be produced at a local station at ten o'clock the following morning.

We took a suburban train out to the station, but the mystery engine had not arrived. Then, at 10.30, a whistle rang out and a swirl of steam appeared 'way down the line. As the speck grew larger it became obvious that it was a British tender engine running backwards. At several hundred metres her rounded cylinders dropped, footplating and lovely curved splashers were diagnostic. It was a 12A. I actually cheered; it was one of the most exciting moments in thirty-five years with railways.

She was No 3826, complete with, 'Beyer Peacock, Manchester, England 1907', embossed on a brass plate that curved over the central splasher. Her lineage was pure Great Central and images of industrial Manchester welled up before my eyes despite the bright sunny morning and azure skies of Bahia Blanca.

Our work done, we returned to Buenos Aires and bade farewell to Hector. We recited our adventures to the Campbells, Richard was saddened by the low ebb to which steam had sunk. 'I doubt it will last the year out', he said gloomily. We now had a few days' rest to be fortified by Mrs Campbell's superb cooking, while arrangements were made for our next adventure – two months in neighbouring Brazil.

BRAZIL

Convinced that our blue flash bulbs contained narcotics the 'Chefe do Frontiere' broke two open to taste their insides.

We reached the Brazilian border in a jaded stupor after a two-day bus journey from Buenos Aires. Everyone heaped out their cases for inspection; we placed ourselves last in the queue in view of the large amount of photographic supplies we carried. The first case the inspector opened was full of heavy-duty flash bulbs. Staring at the dazzling array he jabbered noisily in Portuguese with a pained expression. The same happened with the next case, and he became increasingly animated. The floor was soon covered with bulbs and having smelt, tapped and licked them, convinced that they contained narcotics, the unhappy man disappeared to seek advice. By the time he reappeared with two aides, half the passengers had disembarked to help us and a battle of words took place. The issue was won by two stout Brazilian ladies with whom we had shared chocolate the night before. They were little short of hitting the officials with umbrellas before they relented and let us through.

We continued through a brilliant green landscape, enclosed by bald sugar-loaf hills scattered with naked grey stones. Craggy trees protruded from the rocky pinnacles, and crimson soil appeared through the blanket of tropical undergrowth like flesh wounds in a huge, green, furry animal. A clouded sky was awash with shades of semi-luminous grey, whilst bursts of radiant sunlight illuminated distant grasslands into bands of gleaming colour. As we travelled the winding road, the position of a crimson and ruddy flowering tree moved past varying green backgrounds until it rotated before an area of vermilion soil and the combination exploded into an orgasm of colour.

Sao Jose's lovely Sharp Stewart 4-4-0. When she was exported from Glasgow, Queen Victoria had another ten years to rule the British Empire.

After arriving in Rio we transferred to Campos, in readiness for work on the sugar plantations. During the first week we were guests of Dr Inojosa and his wife Dona Angela who owned the Usina Outeiro and St Pedro distillery that processed sugar cane into the alcohol on which quite a number of road vehicles run. The doctor was the president of Copperflu, a co-operative that embraced eleven of the seventeen sugar factories in Campos state. Collectively they had a marvellous fleet of engines, mainly American, ranging from small tank classes to Moguls 2-8-0s and Mikados. From Outeiro, we visited Usina São José where a gorgeous Sharp Stewart 4-4-0 No 5 with a huge brass dome was in operation. Dated 1892 she was already 86 years old, and a great tribute to the Springburn builders.

São José's siding connects with the Rio to Campos main line, and one evening we set off down the plantation branch dragging with us heavy cases of lighting equipment for a night session of photographing No 5 making her last haul up to the factory that day. On the way we watched golden hills and blazing cane fields melting into a crimson sunset. It was dark when we reached the loading siding and the clear sky showed many constellations, as well as a lovely view of the Milky Way. A new moon rose and bats, owls, frogs, moths and fireflies came out in profusion. We sat in the pitch blackness for two hours before deciding that the engine would not come. Quite apart from missing the picture we were relying on No 5 to get us back to Campos. Reluctantly we packed up the equipment and began the long walk up to the main line. We had stumbled about a kilometre or so when a whistle sounded and exhaust beats became audible. We stopped, listening to the lovely sounds until, far away, a light appeared. It was the Sharp Stewart drifting through the tropical Brazilian night. As she approached we waved our torch and shouted. She stopped and we clambered onto the footplate. In the event, there was ample time to make the picture and No 5 remained in the siding for over an hour before departing with the loads. We reached the junction with the main line at midnight, and waited for the overnight express from Campos to Rio before proceeding.

Our engine rode superbly over the Federal Railway's excellent track, the driver had been on duty for fifteen hours, and the smooth running combined with the warm tropical night, and heat of the footplate, caused him to fall asleep. The fireman, though managing to stay awake to maintain boiler pressure was equally fatigued by the back breaking job of loading logs into the firebox by hand. Travelling on a main line at night with the driver fast asleep was a completely new experience, and as we approached Campos around 2.30am I felt uneasy about the level crossing. The lights of occasional road vehicles could be seen in the distance. With the fireman almost dozing off himself, the best I could do was to keep blowing No 5's glorious deep toned whistle, which did little to alert our crew but hopefully gave some warning to the road ahead. We finally ran into Campos Station yard at 2am. As we dismounted and prepared to return to our hotel, we left the Sharp Stewart simmering in the yard with her magnificent brass dome glinting under the station lamps; an apparition from a bygone age.

Far to the south lay another great centre of steam activity, for the town of Tubarão is host to the magnificent Teresa Cristina Railway. This system is isolated from the rest of Brazil's railway network and was 100 per cent steam operated. A last refuge of American steam superpower, the Teresa Cristina has the last surviving Texas type 2-10-4s. The railway's function is to carry coal from nearby mines, either to feed the giant Capivari Power Station, or for shipment from the docks at Imbituba on the Atlantic Coast. The 2-10-4s head down from the mines with 1,800 ton trains, sometimes reaching speeds of 96km/h. The returning rakes of empties are almost a half mile long. Upon arrival in Tubarão we were befriended by the operations' chief, Sn Antonio Costa Netto, who had us to dinner every evening and co-ordinated activities for us. Neither he nor his wife Cecilia could speak a word of English, and yet, communications with them

'The Sunday Stoker'. An array of gently simmering giants awaiting the new week's workings from Tubarão.

were clearer than with many people at home. By simply drawing a sketch, or acting a little charade, Costa understood us with great clarity.

Our days began before dawn and I would walk through the deserted streets of Tubarão down to the shed for the first departures. Having joined an engine, we ran light through the suburbs, the clonking wheels and whistle blasts arousing residents in lineside houses from their slumber as leaving an enormous black smoke trail in our wake, we ran up to the triangle to collect empty wagons.

On some mornings I took a turn at driving, and the willingness of the Texas 2-10-4 to respond to every slight pressure on the regulator was akin to that of a thoroughbred racehorse at the jockey's gentle tap of the whip. The line headed out across an enormous expanse of marshland, and at kilometre 61 the train stopped for me to disembark. Through the early light came a fine variety of American-built motive power heading trains up to the mines; Texas 2-10-4s, Mikados, a 2-8-0 nicknamed 'Grimy Hog', and the big four-cylinder 2-6-6-2 Mallets. The marsh provided a full vista of the approaching trains in a fine setting. Only one thing spoiled this paradise – the marsh was a breeding ground for mosquitoes. Though quiescent by day, they were still active at first light, and in order to relieve the torment of their bites, I would have to strip off all my clothes and remain naked for about an hour to restore calm. Being naked on the marsh was no embarrassment, as there was not another human being within five kilometres.

The marsh was a huge nature reserve with a steam railway running through the centre. The avifauna ranged from humming birds to vultures, with many species decked in tropical colours. One of the most fascinating was a small bird whose habit was to perch on a lineside post. It would rise into the air, to the height of sixty centimetres whereupon it hovered, sang a jingling little tune, and dropped back onto the post. This process was constantly repeated as if the bird were attached to an invisible cord. I later described this to Costa who laughed, saying it was a 'negro do bumbo' and told how the bird sat on fishermen's rods to give a display and how it was a local practice to move the rod slightly to one side, causing the hapless bird to fall into the water when it attempted to return to its perch.

Long days of lineside photography on the Teresa Cristina, were stimulating yet debilitating. The inevitable miles of walking along the track, carrying tripods and equipment, and looking for the best locations, took a very heavy toll in the steamy tropical heat. But by the third week, I had progressed far enough to examine the Rio Florita branch, which included Sideropolis Tunnel, a green oasis and a fine photographic location. Its cool shady entrance was like passing from a sauna into an airconditioned room. Water sprayed from the rocks above the tunnel mouth and cascaded down amid exotic green fronds, providing invigorating cool showers. Here Stephanie and I bathed freely,

Grimy Hog *crosses the marsh with a train of empties bound for the mines.*

protected by the long narrow tunnel on one side and a large rock cutting on the other.

One afternoon, Costa and I positioned ourselves on the triangle next to the overgrown site of the original roundhouse, in order to photograph one of the Baldwin Mallets. She looked magnificent easing her train onto the triangle; a superb pall of smoke curled lazily from the chimney as the giant whistled impatiently for the road. We ran up to the engine for some exciting photography but no sooner had I fired the shutter than shouts came from the footplate and the crew began to throw lumps of coal in my direction. Suddenly Costa pushed me sharply forwards with a lightning action. Surprise turned to horror, as, within a couple of metres from where I had been standing, an enormous black snake was rearing out of the tangled undergrowth. The colour drained from my cheeks and my legs turned to jelly as the driver and fireman ran towards us with a shovel and a fire rake. They slashed the grass viciously but the creature had disappeared into the thickets. The sombre expression on the men's faces left me in no doubt of the tragedy that had been averted.

At twilight the last trains came through from the mines and usually a main liner would be held at the triangle whilst empties came into the loop from Capivari. The black blobs of locomotive smoke drifting against an orange halflit sky were beautifully atmospheric in the gathering stillness of evening. Throaty coughs from 'Grimy Hog' as she moved wagons around the yard, mixed with calls from flocks of querulous birds winging their way to roosting grounds. Then the soft buzzing of mosquitoes heralded the rapidly advancing darkness. The days ended with a late dinner at Costa's and coffee served on the verandah. Sounds of stragglers running light from the marshalling yard could be heard above the engines simmering quietly in the depot. Costa knew which engine was coming in simply by the tone of its whistle; he could even identify the driver by the way the whistle was blown. Such nuances were not surprising as the Teresa Cristina was his life; he had grown up with the engines.

Several of the Texas type had particularly distinctive exhaust beats and Costa would entertain us by imitating them. One, No 305, had a gruff, sore-throated bark, and he would write the number on a pad before imitating the sound. As the engines came into the depot, the rolling and banging of their motion set up a lovely rhythm. This approximated phonetically to 'café-compon-mantegenon', which in Portuguese, means 'coffee with bread but no butter', and in order to communicate this, Costa did a lovely charade with a coffee pot, loaf of bread, and butter, moving them around the table to the sounds of the engines.

It was now close to Christmas. Santa Claus and Rudolph toured Tubarão, their snowy attire looking incongruous in the balmy tropical heat. We had to decide whether to spend Christmas with Costa and his family. Time dictated we should move on; we had been in Tubarão almost a month and after a tearful farewell we set off overland for Paraguay.

PARAGUAY

It was Christmas Eve when Stephanie and I arrived in Asunción, the capital of Paraguay. Having settled into an hotel, we went down to the shed. Four locomotives were in steam, a Yorkshire Engine Company Mogul of 1953 named *Asunción*, a Hawthorn Leslie 2-6-2 tank of 1910, with a distinct LB and SCR flavour, a North British-built 4-6-0, and a Baldwin 2-8-0, both purchased from Argentina's Urquiza Railway. There was no finer Christmas present than the sight of four such vintage engines simmering majestically in the ancient depot.

Paraguay's great attraction was the all-steam main line which runs to the Argentinian border at Encarnación, so providing through services to Buenos Aires. Known grandly as the 'Ferrocarriel Presidente Carlos Antonio Lopez', the line is 371km long and has changed little since its construction by Edwardian engineers. We left Asunción on Christmas Day bound for Sapucaí where the railway works were situated.

Our train had nine bogie coaches, decked in lovely brown livery including a restaurant car and fairly comfortable first-class accommodation. But the system was desperately the worse for wear. Trains had no brakes, and the track was appalling – held together more by soil and weeds than by nuts and bolts, whilst rotten sleepers confined our speed to a crawl. The railway was under British ownership until 1961, when it was nationalised. In celebration the new administration applied large 'Republica del Paraguay' emblems to the engine's smokebox doors.

Sapucaí is a tiny village some eighty kilometres from Asunción. Few roads serve the area, and the village streets comprise grassy avenues bordered by flowering trees. With no electricity, it seemed an incongruous choice for a locomotive works. The erecting shop resembled that of a British locomotive builder from the nineteenth century. The complete works, every drill and lathe, was activated by steam provided by three stationary boilers standing in the overgrown works yard, having been taken from withdrawn engines. But the pride of Sapucaí was a huge steam hammer from Thwaites Bros Vulcan Ironworks, Bradford, Yorkshire. Every lunchtime the factory hooter resounded lazily over the sleepy village; it might have been Bolton at the turn of the century. The colonial atmosphere of the works offices had to be experienced to be believed – ancient typewriters, Victorian desks, dusty files – all reminded one of a Britain long past.

Our accommodation in Sapucaí was Spartan, a room with bare walls and camp beds on a dirt floor. With no guide, communication was extremely difficult, and the villagers were indifferent to our presence. Sapucaí ran to its own timeless rhythms. The entire village took siesta in the lazy heat haze and at five in the afternoon the works closed, industry fell silent and a chorus of treebugs took over. In the evening all would sojourn to drink maté in front of their houses, as dense flocks of martins scurried round the buildings.

Our evenings in Sapucaí were magical; black velvet nights, free from the reflected wash of electricity, highlighted constellations with a resilience unknown and unimaginable to Western urban society. Our boarding house was immediately next to the railway, and I would sit outside in the balmy night air with a cigar and a glass of whisky, watching the Edwardian Moguls expel shrouds of fire high into the sky. A situation which put me as close to paradise as I might reasonably expect to get.

Throughout the night, the lowing of cattle mixed with the sounds of heavy shunting slide-valve engines made a blissful symphony, laced with the crowing of cocks long before the break of dawn. The scourge of this paradise was the mosquitoes; before sleeping we had to cover our entire bodies with repellant and after a hot night would awake feeling horribly sticky, necessitating a head-to-toe wash at the icy cold well in the backyard.

Daybreak revealed a clear dew-speckled earth, and chickens ranged freely round the homesteads while the cows came in for milking.

In such places as Sapucaí, one can think in light vein of multi-storey developments, traffic jams, inflation, rapid pace of living and all attendant neuroses of the West.

From Sapucaí we journeyed the length of the main line to Encarnación. Our engine was Mogul No 103 built by North British in 1910. It took seventeen hours to cover 300km, an average of 17.6km/h, several derailments having extended the delay. The tranquil landscape trickled slowly past the coach windows, and wafts of sweet smelling woodsmoke drifted through the train. Every eighty kilometres or so, the trains have to stop for refuelling. The wood, having been cut haphazardly in lineside villages, is often too thick to go through the engine's firedoor, and the crew have to knock the logs in with a special hammer. Sometimes, the fire goes out in the process. But when the fires are burning, the constant flurry of flames and sparks issuing from the engine's

Asunción, a Yorkshire Engine Company Mogul built in Sheffield in 1953 and named after the Paraguayan capital, waits to leave San Salvador with a passenger train to Encarnacion on the Argentinian border.

Overleaf:
The huge graveyard at Salonika held many famous designs, included here are examples from the old Hapsburg Empire along with famous American and British designs from World War II.
If Henry Moore had produced a sculpture to the passing of the steam age this is how he would have done it. The remains of a JF Mikado in a scrapyard in Inner Mongolia on the Chinese-Russian border.
The wheel has come full circle for this Indian Railway's Mikado built in 1930 by the legendary Clydeside Shipbuilder, Beardmore of Dalmuir. Note the pieces of anatomy lying in the foreground like the bones of some prehistoric beast.

chimneys not only sets fire to the wood in the tender, but also to the wagons of the train as well. When this happens, the guard brings buckets; these are dipped into the engine's tender and the crew stand throwing water over the blazing train.

Intermittently, we passed through beautiful forests, many ravaged by fires caused by the Moguls. Dense woods stood precariously alongside whole areas of blackened ash; trees reduced to grotesque stumps, along with the cindered remains of lineside fences. Contorted strands of barbed wire noosed the burnt remains of posts which creaked eerily in the breeze. Even some of the wooden sleepers had been reduced to ashes. The Paraguayan farmers had long since learnt to plant their prize crops at least a kilometre away from the main line.

The midday heat was sweltering and the locals – if they appeared at all – wore huge sombreros or used umbrellas as protection. Riding on the engine was like travelling in a furnace through a furnace. Three firemen were needed, as behind the tender was a separate log car, from which the wood was thrown onto the back of the tender. The logs were then hurled to the front of the tender, and finally into the firebox. Upon reaching Carmen Station there was no water; the column was completely dry. So we stopped on a bridge over a culvert several kilometres further on and the engine sucked water through a pipe lowered into the trickling muddy stream. It took an hour to fill the tender during which time No 103 hissed and slurped vigorously. We finally reached Encarnación at 2am. A horse and trap took us from the station to the little hotel that was to be our home for the next few days.

Encarnación depot resembled an Irish shed scene from the twenties, with two Hawthorn Leslie tanks in sleepy repose. These engines worked a short branch to the port at Pacucua. Here a woodfired paddle steamer took the rolling stock across the Rio Paraná to the Argentinian side where they continued their journey over the Urquiza Railway to Buenos Aires.

Hundreds of miles away, deep amid the Paraguayan Chaco, another incredible railway survived. Based upon Puerto Casado, it was the last of many lines built to convey mighty quebracho logs from the interior to factories on the banks of the River Paraguay. One type of quebracho is a source of tannin, used in the treatment of leather, and another has a medicinal bark used in treatment of fever – both are Paraguay's export gift to the world. After processing, the tannin was floated hundreds of miles along the River Paraguay to the Atlantic Ocean at Buenos Aires. Our quest to reach Puerto Casado involved a flight from Asunción in a Cessna plane belonging to the Paraguayan military.

When we took off, the plane shook and rattled alarmingly. Stephanie and I

'The Pride of Harbin'. QJ Class Zhoude, named after one of Mao's generals in the communist revolution, waits to leave Harbin with a southbound freight.

were terrified. For one brief moment I questioned the logic of risking my neck for a collection of old steam locomotives. Once airborne, we turned northwards to fly over some of the wildest country on earth. The River Paraguay gleamed silver as it curved through dense forests below and provided a sure bearing. At intervals I spotted disused track beds radiating from derelict factories on the river's banks and running for miles into the interior in dead straight lines. After several hours we reached our destination and made an unceremonious landing amid a sea of mud on a field airstrip. The humidity hit us like a damp sheet and within minutes began to drain our energy. The temperature was a devastating 42°C and matters were made worse by a recent· invasion into the area of tarantula spiders.

An old Volkswagen track car came rumbling along the seventy-six-centimetre line to collect passengers. There were no proper roads in Puerto Casado, and only three vehicles. We were taken to the company's large rambling guest house, which the tropical trees and plants were threatening to submerge. Living in Puerto Casado was frugal but little shops along the waterfront served warm bread, and cheese soufflés made with maize and eggs. Industry was low key, but the wildness was interrupted by the wail of locomotive whistles or by the clatter of a steam crane. The next day we were awoken before dawn by the hooter of the monthly supply ship coming up the River Paraguay from Asunción.

Down at the running shed we found a wonderful variety of motive power, primarily German, including an attractive 0-4-0 well tank named *Laurita*. She bore an emblem proclaiming her to have been the first steam loco to work on the Paraguayan Chaco, and had come from Arthur Koppel of Berlin in 1898. But the pride of the fleet was *Don Carlos*, a brass-domed 2-8-2 well tank from Manning Wardle. The high spot of the visit was a trip out with *Don Carlos* on the main line, taking empties out into the forest to bring back a loaded train. We set off through a red sunrise, passing the eerie silhouettes of the steam cranes along the riverside. The huge supply boat was now waiting to leave for its long journey back to Asunción. It was fully lit up and in the early light looked like a scene from a romantic film on the Mississippi.

As we headed into the forest, the red flowers on the huge quebracho trees were bursting open as the temperature rose. The Paraguayan Chaco is one of the wonderlands of wildlife left on earth. Whenever the train stopped, huge eagles perched along the wagons, whilst the air was alive with a myriad of flying insects. *Don Carlos* stopped at the loading sidings and hordes of Chaco-bred Indians came up to the engine to see the strange pale-faced visitors. Poverty and shortage of creature comforts there may be in Paraguay, but the people are far richer for having left the wonders of creation intact. What an appalling indictment this wild scrubland proclaims on the overdeveloped, overpopulated nations of the West.

Don Carlos *and crew take a break in the balmy heat amid the wilds of the Paraguayan Chaco.*

In Paraguay, no trains need a whistle after dark as the engines, throwing shrouds of crimson embers thirty metres into the air, are visible from a distance of several kilometres; and to see the ember-throwing veterans dragging their heavy trains into the factory, the tracksides shimmering in a vivid orange glow, constituted steam railroading beyond my wildest imagination. In one of the remotest places on earth I rediscovered, as if through the eyes of a child, the allconsuming magic of a steam train.

All too soon our sojourn in this paradise came to an end and we were back on the muddy airstrip to meet the Cessna. Twenty-four hours later Stephanie and I were on a Rapido bus bound for Buenos Aires and the Campbells. It had been three months since we left Temperley. Now we would return for a few days before proceeding on the next section of our adventure, amid the British-built railways of Uruguay.

URUGUAY

The hydrofoil ploughed its way across the Rio de la Plata from Buenos Aires to Montevideo, and docked in a whirl of technology. The city had a European atmosphere. Skies were grey, and cries of news vendors and traders drifted along streets bustling with raincoats and umbrellas. American cars of twenties Prohibition styling – Chevrolets and Ford Ts, some with wooden wheels – rattled proudly past.

But the railways were entirely British, a home from home as the pre-nationalisation companies echoed the Motherland; Central, Midland, North-Western and Northern. Walking beneath the awe-inspiring portals of Montevideo's Central Articas Station, it was hard to believe that it was not St Pancras, despite the antiquated rolling stock. Yet the station had a rundown atmosphere; there were less trains than there should have been.

Stephanie and I took a suburban train to see the pride of Bella Vista sheds, the unique 4-4-4 tanks, a concept of Edwardian England which flowered but briefly. These examples were the only ones left on earth, and three stood derelict in the yard. Another was discovered in use as a stationary boiler in a small building on the opposite side of the main line. We peered inside to behold a hissing apparition, exuding wisps of steam. Forlornly dismembered, she loomed phantomlike out of the gloom; the last pathetic glimpse of a supremely elegant phase of locomotive development.

With this pitiful image still vivid, we took a diesel-hauled train to Paysandú, a steam centre in the north-west of Uruguay. The journey was predictably slow. We travelled over the vast cattle-rearing plains and saw innumerable loading points at which the beasts were conveyed for the famous meat-canning port of

Fray Bentos on the Rio de la Plata. The track was rough, and poorly maintained; closed stations, and engine sheds, along with abandoned sidings and rusty water columns all intimated that the railway had the same story to tell as that of Uruguay's bigger neighbour across the river.

The railways of Latin America were a vast and invaluable infrastructure, brought about through British enterprise. Their destruction over recent years could not have been more effective had an enemy bombed them into oblivion. In the case of Uruguay, a fifth column had infiltrated railway management, intent on running down the network to a point of inoperability, in order to develop private road services.

The locomotive sheds at Paysandú held nineteen engines, embracing seven classes, all from Beyer Peacock. The oldest was a 2-6-0 tank of the 1880s; the most recent, a pair of Z class Moguls exported in 1929. These were particularly fascinating, having a London and North-Western type smokebox door; the most numerous were the N class Edwardian Moguls, but the pride of Paysandú were the T class 2-8-0s. One survivor, No 139, named *Ing Pedro Magnou*, was on shed in steam; she was the type of engine one would have found in the Scottish Highlands during the thirties, except that this example had a brass nameplate on the side of her Belpair firebox – I'd never seen a nameplate in that position before. The other surviving T class came on shed; No 138 named *Ing V.B. Sudriers*. She carried a plate saying 'Reconstructed 1938 Penarol'. Both engines were named after famous Uruguayan engineers from the Central Railway.

We spent an entire Sunday in Paysandú sheds. Most of the engines were dead, lying mottled in sunbeams which filtered through the broken slats of the old shed roof. The two Ts stood side by side, dormant companions in the silence of the sooty depot, undisturbed save for the occasional dripping of water from an injector pipe and whirling clatter of pigeons in the roof. Outside in the yard stood N class Mogul No 88 of 1906 and further down the last surviving Z Mogul, No 225, sunlight rippling the rusty tones of her North-West smokebox front. I felt as if I were in a time vacuum, for nowhere on earth was a shed full of such diverse British thoroughbreds, whose average age pre-dated World War I. In retrospect, that Sunday has acquired tremendous significance, for homespun British steam did not die in 1968, but survived long after in far-flung Uruguay.

Our return to Montevideo heralded the beginning of a journey from the Atlantic to the Pacific, and Chile's Atacama Desert, a vast inhospitable terrain where rain never falls and where the British built hundreds of kilometres of railway to carry nitrates and gold from the desert to ports on the Pacific Coast. It was to these railways that the legendary Kitson Meyer articulated engine was sent in considerable numbers. Survivors were said to exist in the Atacama but little did we imagine the adventure lying ahead as we waited for the flight from Montevideo to the Chilean capital, Santiago.

CHILE

Our first task in Santiago was to obtain information about the last Kitson Meyers, which operated from the Pacific port of Taltal, hundreds of miles to the north. But the Chilean Ministry of Chemicals and Minerals, told us the system had closed and was being dismantled. Shattered by the news I determined to put on film whatever was left of the Taltal Railway. We boarded a Pan American highway bus in Santiago which would drop us in the middle of the desert, twenty-four kilometres from Taltal. Somehow we would make our way onwards to the coast.

Heading northwards, the green landscape gave way to barren rock; the Andes were to the east, the Pacific Ocean to the west. We passed exotic expanses of rocky coastline, almost entirely devoid of human settlements. Upon entering the desert, golden hills soared up against a dark blue sky; the mystique and beauty of this vast uninhabited expanse was awe-inspiring. After twenty hours of travelling, we reached our destination. The bus drew up amid a swirl of dust, leaving us at the roadside, gazing at the little road which led from the Pan American to Taltal. We began to walk expecting to reach our destination by dark, but progress was slower than expected and when a truck approached from the rear we frantically signalled it down to be hauled aboard by a gang of swarthy labourers. 'Taltal' – which means 'place of many stones' – was the only word we could utter. They understood – and yes, there was a 'residencia' which took in guests.

Taltal was like a Nevada ghost town. Partly dismantled buildings, abandoned jetties, derelict storesheds, and rusted rail sidings. It was as if some holocaust had struck a once thriving community.

We were welcomed at the 'residencia' and given a room overlooking the Pacific. Before dinner I searched the little town for the railway. I had tried to question the landlord about it but all he could say was '*finito*', his expression clearly indicating the hardship Taltal had suffered as a result of losing its industry.

The huge railway yards and workshop lay behind several padlocked gates. The Victorian home of the former general manager stood as proud as ever, overlooking the works. Tracks had been lifted and no engines were visible. A horrible feeling seeped into my bones. I was too late, the Kitson Meyers were extinct. The huge engine shed with its holding capacity for more than thirty locomotives had been pulled down around the few surviving engines in sight, which were covered in bricks and old rafters. There were two Kitson Meyers. One was jacked up for an overhaul which had never been completed and the other's boiler had exploded. All around the shed entrance were pieces of cut-up locomotives; it was the boneyard of the Kitson Meyer. On the way back to the hotel I stopped at the abandoned offices; time clocks still adorned the office walls, frowning down, echoing their past age of discipline and severity. Amid a heap of dust and papers lay a *Girls' Annual of 1912.*

Feeling depressed Stephanie and I ate supper in silence and we had barely finished when the landlady came in, saying, 'Anglais, Senor, Anglais'. An Englishman in Taltal? Surely not! A small boy was summoned to guide us to a house a short distance away. As we approached, the sound of a Chopin piano sonata carried through the still atmosphere. My spirits fell when a Chilean lady who spoke no English opened the door, but as we entered, the music stopped and a tall elderly man with a 1920s style moustache rose from the piano. 'Good evening', he said with a faint London accent, 'you're just in time for the BBC World Service'. 'You're English!' 'English? – I was born in Tottenham in 1899, I'm Eric Ridpeth. I'm 80. I came here in 1921 to work for Anglo-Chilean Nitrates on the Taltal Railway, and lived here ever since. What is your business here?' 'The Kitson Meyers', I replied. His face darkened. 'There is no railway here any more.' 'But Taltal has the last . . .' 'There is no railway'. Eric retorted sharply, 'Only a wreck. I spent my life with that railway, it was one of the finest in the world, now it has been destroyed'.

To us of a different age, Eric seemed autocratic, narrow minded and disciplinarian. Yet the essence of his behaviour and his kind not only produced the finest empire the world had ever seen, but produced a manufacturing and production process of development and achievement which is the envy of today's easygoing free-for-all world. 'I'll never seen England again', he confided. 'Some day I'll join my old colleagues in the British Cemetery upon the nearby hill. I love Taltal; I have everything here I could wish for'.

It was very difficult to get Eric to talk about the railway – he had, after all, seen it ruined before his eyes. Eventually, he admitted that ten Kitson Meyers had come to Taltal. 'Only No 59 still survives', he shrugged dismally, 'the one that was fitted with the Robinson superheater back in the twenties'. 'Only 59?' I queried. 'Yes, she stands down by the beach'. 'You mean one is complete?' I said. 'Just one; Señor Acosta, the last manager used it on demolition work, but that was a long time ago. It will never work again. It belongs to the past. It's not fit to work, it has stood out in the sea air for years.' We left with surging spirit and I could hardly sleep for excitement. By seven the next morning I was banging on Acosta's door. He accompanied us to a line hugging the shore and there in all its magnificence was No 59 – the dodo of the Atacama. Now came the vital question, could Acosta make it work for one last pictorial session? Yes, he said, it could work after repairs had been effected; it would take two days.

We visited Eric to tell him of our plans. 'I will have nothing to do with it', he said. 'You are advised to leave that engine well alone; it's as rotten as a bad pear. It belongs to the past. It will blow up on Acosta. You will see'. We tried to explain that if we got these pictures, they would provide a permanent memory of the Taltal Railway, but he was unrepentant. Sad that we had lost an ally, we

The Dodo of the Atacama breathes her final gasps as she heads out of Taltal. Seconds later, the engine disappeared beneath a geyser of water and escaping steam.

left, and by first light were down at the beach. Two men were plugging up the leaking tubes whilst a third was busy on the exhaust pipe. They had worked all night and by evening the repairs would be completed. And Acosta, with a smile all over his face announced that the engine would be in steam by the following afternoon.

At 11.30 the next morning the long years of waiting ended. The fire was lit and my journey halfway across the world had borne fruit. As we moved the Kitson Meyer around the yard she emitted a gorgeous panting sound; shrouds of dark oil smoke swirled from her front chimney, whilst her rear one sent clouds of pure white steam up into the sky. Then without warning, a geyser of scalding water issued from the engine's leading chimney. Acosta dived for cover and the exploding dodo disappeared in a shroud of wet steam and boiling water. We were lucky nobody was killed, and in the midst of this terrible trauma I noticed a tall, elderly figure silently watching through a distant gate. Acosta was unrepentant, 'It will take another day', he said, 'but we must let her cool down'. There was nothing more to do that day, so we returned to the residencia.

The beauty of the Pacific Coast contrasted with the arid desert and never before had I seen so many fish brought from the sea by individuals. With Taltal's industry closed, the residents were increasingly dependent upon fish as a major source of food and Taltal's fishermen do a morning round of the houses with a huge array of different fish suspended from wooden shoulder yokes.

The following afternoon, steam was up again and once more the Meyer began to run around the yard. We collected some wagons and prepared to make a run out of the works area, towards the hills. But before photography could begin, the engine started to make a peculiar noise which began as a strange throaty bubbling of ever increasing intensity. The crew rapidly brought the engine to a standstill, jumped from the cab, and put as much distance between themselves and No 59 as possible. No sooner had they done this than the gurgle erupted into a ferocious rushing sound and the engine disappeared from view in a roaring ball of steam, as if the boiler itself had exploded. Acosta looked embarrassed; he had done everything humanly possible to coax the dodo back to life.

Not only was the engine unsteamable, but also extremely dangerous. Even I would have been prepared to call it a day, but Acosta's eyes were full of defiance. 'We will repair it tomorrow', he said calmly, and sure enough, forty-eight hours later, the Meyer had steam yet again. The veteran picked up her wagons and headed away through the derelict works towards Breas. It was as if the whole of Taltal had come to life once again, No 59's lovely chimney-whistle echoing plaintively around the town, a sound guaranteed to strike a chord in the heart of every resident. Young and old alike flocked to the old works area to see the dodo resurrected.

It was a triumph of determination to reach that wild place, a triumph of a railway manager to accede to our request and a triumph of the steam locomotive, invariably able to turn a wheel, no matter how great the odds. Now the final triumph was for me to put it onto film for all time.

The end of the expedition had come and throughout our long journey back to Britain, I was conscious only of images; Paraguayan woodburners, with flames flung thirty metres into a velvet black night; the virility of the last Texas type 2-10-4s, highballing along at nearly 100km/h with their mighty trains. But, overshadowing all, the dodo of the Atacama, a lost species, gasping her final breath in that wild waterless desert. The expedition – like a dream – crystallised into a heightened feeling of wonderment, which to this day, almost ten years later, remains an integral part of my thinking and very being.

·10·
Photography

A nightingale sang in the wooded grounds and the summer evening was warm and still. Dinner had been excellent, served in a dining room overlooking Lyme Regis Bay. The initial session of a week's residential photography course was about to begin. Relaxed and contented the students filed into the conference room. I began with customary attack.

'Why are we here?' Everyone looked blank.

'Learning to take pictures', one wag chirped.

'Of what?' There was no answer.

'You don't come on a Colin Garratt course to be woolly-headed. Why are we here?' Expressions revealed that the students had been expecting a cosy social evening.

'Photography is seldom relaxing', I informed them, 'stimulating yes, but you must be permanently on your mettle if you are to become photographers of any value'.

My immediate task was to encourage a positive approach; to present a challenge.

'You are all individual, you look different, think differently, write differently, so why are your photographs indistinguishable from one another's? A painter's work is characteristic, so should yours be as a photographer'. I then wrote on the blackboard, in huge letters: 'RMA'.

'This stands for Right Mental Attitude'. Their indigestion was complete.

Throughout that week RMA watched over us like big brother since an agreement was reached that anyone not adopting the right mental attitude to his photography would be named and charged at our evening meetings. Intimidating? Certainly. But the students had paid a lot of money to take the course and I was determined that their photography should improve!

We projected sets of transparencies to assess four basic elements in picture formation.

Form one of the first things we have to learn as photographers is how to place, forms or shapes harmoniously within a scene.

Light photographers model with light as a potter models with clay and many use it as the main theme of a picture.

Colour if the emphasis is not on light then it may be on colour.
Effect many pictures are primarily concerned with visual effects to create atmosphere, such as silhouettes or sunsets.

Simple criteria, although the four elements often merge in varying degrees. Studying these components has trained me to read pictures as words and so understand what the pictorialist is saying.

The major problem facing aspiring photographers is that of composition. Quite apart from selecting the best angle for a picture, we have to decide what to include and what to leave out, whilst being aware of not only the subject, but its relationship with surroundings as well. We studied the rule of thirds; the balancing of masses; the role of colour in weighting a composition convincingly; use of foreground detail; incompatible elements in pictures and more obvious aspects like the use of planes from foreground to middle-distance and background.

Outdoor practical sessions included two days working on a pre-set route through the countryside, embracing noteworthy churches, picturesque villages, magnificent sweeps of landscape, coastline, and even industrial earthworks. Watching the students approach their subjects was fascinating. Some took viewpoints from the easiest place of access, others crashed through hedges, jumped brooks and climbed trees, whilst one member got his head down and charged a herd of cows to clear them from the scene. *Contra-jour* vied with other oblique angles as subjects were interpreted from all points of the compass through a battery of lenses, ranging from 20mm to 300mm. The results of these practicals were processed overnight by Agfa, screened and analysed and we all learned a great deal from them.

Back in the classroom for a session called 'How not to do it' in which I projected some atrocious colour transparencies. Many of the errors were obvious like the one of the girl with a giant teasel growing out of her head – once seen never forgotten! A little more subtle was a family portrait on the lawn in which we were treated to a view of the dustbin, a pair of knickers on a line in the background, an ugly pole protruding from the side and almost half a mile of foreground. It is easy to undermine an elegant theme by inadvertently creating a cluttered mire of shape and colour.

A practical aspect always demonstrated on these courses is 'Learning to see again' – a theme that has given me endless enlightenment and pleasure. It involves taking a set scene from a specified camera viewpoint at different times over successive days. Nature is in a constant state of change, her moods and colours can vary minute by minute and the interpretation of these infinite moods provides photography with much of its fascination. As an example I always project a remarkable trio of pictures taken by Monica on one of her practicals back in 1970. The scenes depict a field of yellow rape, a church on the horizon and a mass of open sky. In the first picture the sun is shining obliquely on the church, and although it is beautifully lit, the cloud patterns are uninspiring. The next picture, taken some days later, has a much more impressive sky and may be thought of as the finest rendition of the scene possible. That is until the third variation is produced, taken after a storm. The sky has turned steely-grey; the sun continues to illuminate both rape and church, but now there is a glorious rainbow, and in the interim a flag had been set on the flagpole of the steeple. The storm lighting, rainbow and billowing flag produced a breathtaking picture which shows how by observation and perception, the photographer – like the painter – can transform normal scenes into unforgettable visions, glorifying the beauty of the natural world.

We spent much of that week studying paintings; after all, the greatest railway picture is not a photograph, but a painting: Turner's 'Rain, Steam and Speed'. This masterpiece depicts one of Gooch's broad-gauge Fireflies speeding over the Maidenhead Viaduct during a squally storm in the Thames Valley. Speeds of 90mph – 144km/h – had been reported; man had never travelled so fast and Turner painted this work in celebration. Flaming coals bounce along the track-sides and a hare races for its life ahead of the locomotive, Turner relates the speed of nature with that of the machine. Three puffs of steam issue from the engine's chimney serving to heighten the rate at which the Firefly dashes across the picture, whilst the coaches recede to a breathtaking perspective in the swirling haze. The misty expanse of the Thames Valley includes two horses drawing a plough over a meadow, sedately emphasising the quiet timelessless of centuries gone by. Crowds wave to the passing train from the rainsodden banks of the Thames – railways were still a novelty in 1844 – whilst the present A4 highway leading to London appears obscurely in the background, significantly shrouded in obscurity, for Turner celebrates the advent of the great railway age. Heady stuff indeed. Thackeray, when describing this painting, referred to the amazing appearance of movement the picture has. 'There comes upon you a steam train travelling at 50mph (Thackeray's estimated speed), which the observer had best be quick to see lest the train passes through the wall of the gallery and is away up the Charing Cross Road'.

But the guiding star of my life's ambition as a pictorialist is Turner's immortal painting of the 'Fighting Temeraire'. The hero of Trafalgar and one of Nelson's great fleet, is seen being drawn across the Thames at Rotherhithe to her last mooring place, at which she will be broken up. The *Temeraire* is towed by a brand-new steam tug, jubilantly belching a pall of smoke into the evening sky, the age of steam has dawned and Turner makes distinction between steam and sail. The virility with which the iron-clad leviathan is depicted in contrast with

J.W.M. Turner's 'Rain, Steam and Speed' painted in 1844.
J.W.M. Turner's 'Fighting Temeraire' painted in 1839.

the pallid form of the *Temeraire*, already a phantom from a bygone age, is breathtaking. The caption which Turner appended to the painting read 'The flag which braved the battle and the breeze no longer owns her'. Far better than our physically preserving the *Temeraire* in dry dock, Turner has immortalised her on this incomparable canvas.

The best pictures, whether paintings or photographs, convey that vital association of ideas which reveal the artist's interpretation of reality. If I could make pictures which read like an essay then my ultimate ambition would be fulfilled. This association of ideas is invariably stronger in paintings largely because the photographer has to home in on his subject very tightly in order to honour the basic requirements of form, colour and content.

A picture that takes 1/500sec to shoot can take hours or days of preparation. Enormous discipline and patience is needed as numerous hazards can spoil a picture not least when working with moving subjects like trains. If the trains passed every few minutes many problems could be overcome by a few simple reshoots, but with steam traction there are few busy lines left. If the light on location is good for a certain train, and something goes wrong it is invariably twenty-four hours before a reshoot can be made. The obvious hazard with steam photography is an absence of smoke. Often a whole composition will be based around a smoke trail, whilst all manner of extraneous junk like telegraph poles, wires or ugly buildings can be blotted out by a fine brew from an engine's chimney. The sun often disappears behind passing cloud the second the train reaches the prescribed spot, whilst people – invariably in screaming white shirts – walking into a carefully composed colour composition at the crucial moment are equally ruinous. Wind is either a devoted ally or a saboteur; often, a mischievous wind will lift a speeding train's smoke and deposit it into the wrong area of the picture.

Equally, unexpected lucky breaks give a tremendous boost to photographic morale. One of my pictures took only four days when I had prepared for a siege of ten. It was on a branch line in Slovenia where former German war engines were working. The location faced due west, there were grasses in the foreground, one metre in front of the camera lens, whilst on the horizon the line could be seen crossing an embankment against open sky. The aim was to catch the train with the setting sun just above the locomotive. A tough assignment as weather conditions were variable, the trains spasmodic and the sun only in range for about thirty minutes, not to mention a possible deficiency of smoke which added a further dimension to the equation.

On the first day I took up my position ready for the train, but the sky become overcast and no sunset occurred. The following day was perfectly clear and the sun went down blazing, but no train. On the third day the sun and train coincided perfectly but there was no smoke from the engine. On the fourth day I asked a Yugoslav friend to go one station up the line and brief the fireman to

A picture like this can sometimes take weeks of waiting, but to achieve the right combination of sun, smoke and cloud so quickly, was one of those lucky breaks photographers dream of.

make some smoke at the appropriate spot. Feeling nervous I watched the sun slowly dip towards the horizon but again no train. Within minutes the sun would sink too low for a good composition. 'If only', I thought as I sat chewing my nails in misery. Suddenly, to my indescribable joy, I heard the whistle and minutes later the war engine rolled into the scene, complete with an obliging trail of smoke. Seldom was a camera shutter fired more ecstatically; it is at moments such as these that photography becomes sublime.

There are four questions which arise with unfailing regularity on every course. The most common is 'Which came first – your love of trains or your love of photography?' I like to bounce this question back and ask which the questioner thinks came first. The guesses come equally divided but the answer is unequivocal, railways. For I see photography as a communicative medium, not as an end in itself. Once an individual has something to say he chooses the medium in which he can best express himself. the golden rule being – it's not that we like to photograph, but what do we like enough to want to photograph?

The second question, 'Why are so many of your pictures taken at night?' This question is always disheartening as I feel the pictures ought to provide the answers for themselves. So much of the steam locomotive's inherent potency and magic appears at night and the sight of an iron-clad monster bathed in swirling fire and steam is a natural theme. I remember the awe I felt on seeing Philip de Loutherbourg's paintings of iron foundries at the dawn of the industrial revolution; the emotional atmosphere of the fiery scenes made a deep impression.

The next question is 'What equipment and film do you use?' For the first ten years of my professional life I used the cheapest and simplest camera in the Praktica range; it had no light meter as I preferred to hand set the camera myself having taken a reading from the ever-trusty Weston. Lenses varied from 20mm super wide up to 200mm telephoto but most of the work was done between 28mm and 80mm. 'And film?' Before turning professional I tested various colour films and found Agfa's colour renditioning and tolerance unbeatable. It is imperative that photographers get to know the characteristics of their film. The ultimate tragedy in photography is to be a hopeful button-presser, but by choosing top quality film like Agfa and acquiring an intimate knowledge of it one can look through the camera viewfinder and say with conviction 'I know what this picture will look like when it appears on the screen.' This surely is the creative joy of photography.

The last question belongs to the 'Why don't you?' syndrome: 'WDY take movie films?' 'WDY make sound recordings?' 'WDY do video?' If I were to diversify into other areas requiring totally different techniques, variety would undermine quality. There is wisdom in being true to your cause. I am a believer in the still picture, and regard it as superior to the moving image.

Whatever effort we put into our photography and however we justify that effort, a professional's work will – in the final analysis – be judged by others. The following reviews mirror the years of study and effort expended in attempting to document with eloquence an age which was not just at the core of the industrial revolution but one of tremendous romance as well.

'To define Colin Garratt as a "railway enthusiast" is to deny his higher ranking as an artist.'
'A serious man with a serious task.'
'The David Attenborough of steam locomotives.'
Ian Jack – The Sunday Times

'All his photographs are composed with the care of a landscape painter.'
Jeremy Kingston – The Sunday Express

·11·
India — My Second Home

People often ask which, of all the countries I have visited, is my favourite. The answer is India. Embracing an incredible potpourri of tradition, terrain and climate, spiced with both British culture and Eastern mysticism, India is the ultimate experience for any spirited traveller.

Despite the country's extreme inequalities most Indians lead stoically cheerful, if Spartan, lives. Indian society is positively Dickensian; all outlandish facets of human behaviour are evident, nurtured by a free market economy. Working overseas one invariably feels a little homesick, but when I return to Britain from India, I become homesick for India. How could any red-blooded Briton feel homesick in a country which has Wills Gold Flake cigarettes in yellow packets, porridge on the breakfast menu, and words such as 'bounder' and 'blighter' in its everyday vocabulary?

The building of India's vast railway network was one of the finest achievements in British history. There is a timelessness about rail travel across India. The innate friendliness of one's companions is a constant endearment and at wayside stations the babble of vendors is akin to birds calling in a thicket. A favourite call is '*chaywala chaywala*' – the tea boy carrying black kettles and a tray of locally made clay cups. The bumps and smashes of the little cups flung from the train are a characteristic sound on leaving the station. Then time to sleep in the afternoon heat, followed by a walk to the washroom as relief from the swirling heat and dust. A smoke and then tea is served once again, this time with *samosa* – potato and green chillies fried in batter and wrapped in palm leaves. '*Paan-e-paan*', a vendor cries at station stops, selling the addictive betelnut which, apart from leaving the mouth and lips orange, ensures that red-speckled blobs form on the pavements and platforms from regular spitting out of the fluid. Platters of peanuts glide past the windows; bananas for a penny and packets of glucose biscuits for tuppence – what a magical land!

A man performs grotesque contortions on the adjacent running line, twisting his body into unimaginable shapes before clapping for money to be flung from the train.

Now on the move again, evening beckons and the heat is pulled from the blazing sun like the venom from a sting. A blind musician, led by a small ragged boy, has joined the train to sing his way along its length before the next station is reached. His music, often haunting and beautiful, is always poignant.

Time to look at our map and see how far we have come; glance over the papers and magazines that become common property in an Indian railway compartment, or time for another stroll along the train to study the fascinating tapestry of travellers; from beggars to mystics, cultured Sikhs to farm labourers, and to angelic children with dirty noses; all sleeping, eating, laughing, crying – a richness of humanity laced by whistles from the steam engine far away up front, emitting periodic blobs of smoke across the kaleidoscopic view behind the barred windows of our coach.

As we run now through a deep twilight, dinner is served in the compartment. It was booked two hours previously and telegraphed along the line by the catering vendors – the traveller wants for nothing. Now the bedrolls are set out and by 9.30 everyone in the compartment is settled down, to be lulled to sleep by the syncopated rhythms of our engine. The sun sets on one side of the train and rises in the morning on the other; bed tea is served at 6am. Arrival is accompanied by a glorious feeling of distance, a different province, another world, a new adventure, a journey well done. Yes, India is my second home.

My most important work in India was the documentation of the XC Pacifics. They consisted of fifty engines, built in Lancashire by Vulcan Foundry, and at William Beardmore's Clydeside shipyard in Dalmuir. They looked very similar to Gresley's LNER A3 Pacifics ('Flying Scotsman') of the same period. For many years the XCs were India's most illustrious locomotives, and by the mid-seventies were the only British express passenger locomotives left in world service. The type formed part of the celebrated X series standards exported from Britain during the 1920s for the 5ft 6in-gauge main lines on the sub-continent, and I made three separate pilgrimages to Bengal to record them. In 1976 ten XCs were working from Calcutta's Howrah shed; demoted from top duties they worked locals and semi-fasts along the Eastern Railway main line. It was on this line that I saw my first XC. As the train came into view, an aged gandy dancer (track ganger), having recognised the type of engine, called out with a toothless grin, 'English legacy, Sahib'. And what a legacy! The sensuous beast that throbbed its way towards the camera epitomised the golden age of railways. A ghost of Doncaster, she picked up her ten-coach train and, with a waft of oily sulphur, was gone.

My affection for the XCs led to a second expedition in 1979, by which time all survivors were allocated to Burdwan, ninety-six kilometres north of Calcutta on

'Scrap iron,' Anupam snapped as he jabbed his thumb at the WP. Despite his sentiments these American inspired Pacifics have virtually monopolised India's steam expresses for some forty years and many remain in traffic today.

the main line to Delhi. I struck an immediate rapport with the depot foreman, S. N. Bajpai. I explained the significance of the XCs and proposed that one of Burdwan's examples should be decked in LNER blue in deference to their lineage. Bajpai readily agreed. Shortage of paint meant that the blue had to be mixed with white to eke out the supply. The result was not quite the LNER livery I had hoped for, and when the pictures were later published in *The Sunday Times Magazine*, a letter was sent to the newspaper by Sir Nigel's daughter, Miss Marjorie Gresley, in which she wrote, 'My father's engines were not remotely that colour; the shade of blue is incorrect.'

But the principle was sound and No 22226 looked stunning in her new livery. 'She's yours', Bajpai said, 'we'll put her on the Bolpur pickup for a week, and along with Loco Inspector Anupum Banerjee and Depot Chargehand Santosh Chaudhuri, you can make your pictures'.

So began one of the most memorable weeks of my life. Bolpur was fifty-six kilometres away on the cross-country line to Jamalpur and the pickup collects and sets down wagons at intermediate stations. The country stations are set amid pleasant farmland with rollers and pied kingfishers perched on the lineside wires. Our midday arrival at Bolpur was timed to coincide with the Sahibanj pickup – worked by a WG class engine – so giving a daily all-stations freight service along this important secondary line – a fine example of the proper use of railways.

At the end of each day I walked from the shed to the retiring rooms at Burdwan Station. The chill winter evenings were foggy and power cuts frequent; I might have been in Glasgow during the 1920s, especially with the proliferation of Communist and Socialist posters along every wall in readiness for the forthcoming Bengal elections. I climbed the stone stairs to my room and upon entering lit a candle. The wardrobe and bed loomed out of the dark shadows. Coal smoke carried in the air, a squeaky LNER-type whistle rang out and engines coughed in the darkness. One evening, crossing to my window I was in time to see an XC come in with a workmen's passenger train. Overcome by this brooding atmosphere of an era gone by, I returned to my wooden desk until the power suddenly came on again as the station announcer heralded the arrival of an electrically-hauled express from Calcutta to New Delhi. It was 1979 and I was in India after all.

At Bolpur, I met Bhadu Das, the shoeshine boy who features in my well known picture, 'The Cattle Boy'. The picture was made south of Bolpur where a viaduct crosses a Ganges tributary and since our Pacific was decked in blue and red we searched the market to find clothes of a similar colour for Bhadu to wear. He was a poor boy who spoke no English, but soon acquired a feeling for the photography. Some brilliant manoeuvring from Anupum Banerjee enabled us to occupy the section for half an hour and run the train backwards and for-wards over the viaduct to achieve the perfect combination of Bhadu and the passing train: 'a Bengali cattle boy sitting entranced alongside a tributary of the Ganges as this Indian version of the *Flying Scotsman* rumbled over the arches'.

On our return from Bolpur we always stopped for water at Guskara and the whole team repaired to a nearby teashop for *rasogolla*, a celebrated local sweetmeat. We rejoined the main line at Khana Junction and one evening arrived there late to find the pegs against us. It was 7.30 and almost dark, a hot evening and we all sat out on the open verandah of the brakevan. Khana has no electricity and as the blackness descended the cacophony of frogs from nearby marshes resembled a vast orchestra, above which we had to raise our voices to be heard. It had been a long scorching day; we had left the shed at 6.30 that morning and, apart from the team wanting to get back, our dinner was booked in the station restaurant for 9pm. Anupum chuntered about being stuck there all evening and disappeared into the darkness. He returned ten minutes later looking jubilant. He had spoken to control via the junction signal box and received special dispensation for us to be fitted in on the fast line between expresses but, as Anupum told driver, Sarkar, we had to get moving. I was ecstatic, here was a chance for our Pacific to show what a thoroughbred she was. We got the green light and with everyone on the footplate, the regulator was opened, our Pacific was notched up, and we lunged out into the darkness with fourteen wagons and a brakevan in tow. Once on the electrified line No 22226 galloped along like a runaway racehorse; I saw Anupum's eyes gleaming in the fireglow, whilst Chaudhuri chuckled away to himself. The feeling of power was frightening as we left a black trail of exhaust under the catenaries. The main line was as smooth as glass and our Pacific rode beautifully. We covered the eleven kilometres in less than seven minutes and drew to a halt in Burdwan station at 8.20. Time for a shower before dinner! It had been a perfect day; the railway, my companions, and our locomotive, all of the very finest.

My adventures with the big blue engine over, I left Burdwan with a heavy heart, promising my friends to return before the XCs were finally withdrawn. Back in England a part of me was left in Bengal. There had to be one more visit to get a final set of historic pictures, possibly of an XC in another kind of British pre-nationalised livery. I corresponded with Bajpai and, having received confirmation that XCs survived at Burdwan, returned to Calcutta in February 1981.

The Great Eastern was Calcutta's first hotel, a splendid relic of the British Raj with endless corridors and palatial banqueting rooms. My arrival coincided with one of the dry periods in which the Communist government of West Bengal banned the sale of alcohol. But the head waiter, who sported a superb British moustache and looked as if he would have been more at home on a Bengal tiger hunt, confided discreetly as he brought my coffee, 'In British time, sir, very much whisky drinking!'

Next day I caught the Black Diamond Express, running from Calcutta to the eastern coalfields of Bengal. Bajpai and Chaudhuri met me off the train. The same retiring rooms had been booked, and having deposited my things, we took Bajpai's trolley down to the shed. 'Is the blue engine here?' I asked eagerly; 'No', Bajpai replied, 'she was despatched to Jamalpur for breaking three months ago. Only five XCs survive but I have an engine ready'. We looked her over, she was No 22224 and I remember whispering to Bajpai, 'Is red all right?' He nodded. It would take several days to get her into shape; the cow-catcher and big lamp had to be removed to emphasise her lineage and she had to be scraped and cleaned before painting could begin; but then she would be perfect, ours for a whole week on the Bolpur pickup.

I loved Burdwan station; its sounds, atmosphere and smells. The mornings dawned sunny and from the platform vendor I would purchase *The Times of India* to read with my cornflakes. The restaurant manager, in typical fashion, tried hard to please and apart from producing traditional breakfasts, would look after me with fish and chip dinners and specially made caramels, which he called custards. Only one detail marred mealtimes – the restaurant cat, which brought in mice, lizards, frogs and cockroaches and consumed them in front of me as I ate.

Soon the red Pacific was ready. She could be seen glowing in the depot yard almost a kilometre away – the next day she would be in steam.

But the following morning I was woken by Bajpai holding a telegram from Eastern Railway HQ in Calcutta. It instructed immediate condemnation of all remaining XCs and their dispatch to Jamalpur works for breaking up. 'We are being given WGs to replace them', Bajpai said, 'and the first two are arriving light-engine today. I knew nothing about it until I reached the office this morning'.

We called a meeting at the shed at 10am with Anupum Banerjee, Chaudhuri and the divisional manager. Dare we run No 22224 'on line' when officially condemned? The urgency of the telegram stemmed from the need for non-ferrous materials, especially copper fireboxes. The glint in Chaudhuri's eye brightened as he lifted a file from an adjacent cabinet – by amazing coincidence our engine was the only one with a steel firebox. This clinched the matter and we agreed to take the risk and run our engine for one week on the Bolpur pickup. We all knew the chance we were taking; if anything went wrong there could be serious repercussions from Calcutta HQ. What an incredible coincidence that the telegram had arrived on the very morning the programme was due to begin.

So began another week of non-stop adventure with the team I had in 1979. Everyone got on well and all of us felt a sense of history. During this time the withdrawn sister engines were dispatched light or in pairs to Jamalpur. One evening, returning from Bolpur, we passed No 22216 dragging No 22204. They had stopped as No 22216's tubes were leaking so badly that she was preparing

```
NO  9


XXR  1600   CCC    5

DME / P  HWH  C/ ACME  / W/JMP  CO S / CCC  DY  COS/ ?  JMP

LF / BWN  HLO  CPNL  HWH

NO M 99/1/  S  VOL  VIII  AAA  ALL  XC  CLASS  LOCOS  HAVE  BEEN

OFFERED  TO  COS  CCS+ CCC  FOR  DISPOSAL  THROUGH  AUCTION

AFTER  OBTAINING  GM/S  SANCTION  ON  11 TH / 12 TH  INSTANT

AAA  LOCOS  WITH  COPPER  FIV+  FIRE  BOXES  TO  BE  SEND  TO

JMP  SHOP  IMMEDIATELY  SO  AS  TO  REACH  SHOP  BY  7 TH  INSTANT

AS  L+  ALREADY  ADVISED  AND  SEND  LF  BWN  WITH  DETAILS  OF

WEIGHT  OF  COPPER  AND  NONFERROUS  MATERIALS  ETC  TO  COS  CCC

ON  7 TH  INSTANT  POSITIVELY  AAA  CMPE / RL  /  CCC

CMPW+  CMPE  ( PL )



HWH  BWN     0035   6TH
```

The telegram from the Eastern Railway's HQ in Calcutta condemning the last XC Pacifics. Included is the allusion to non-ferrous metals.

to return to Burdwan for attention, leaving No 22204 dumped in the station yard at Khana.

I usually travelled footplate, and once we left the main line at Khana, locals could be seen standing close to the track with forked branches into which were tucked various denominations of rupees. This is a classic Indian ruse to get coal, the principle being that the driver snatches the money and the fireman heaves over the appropriate amount of coal. This practice is rife on India's secondary lines and is one of the reasons why steam traction is regarded as expensive, for as much as two tons of coal can be sold in this way on an average run. Driver Sarkar was not party to this practice but on one of the days we had another driver; with Anupum Banerjee on the footplate no sales could be made, to the chagrin of the blank-faced locals. That afternoon I noticed our engine smoking heavily whenever we were not on the footplate, and later during the return run we were riding in the brakevan and a very unhealthy sound was coming from the engine; she was being throttled. I told Anupum that something was wrong. 'Nothing', he replied grimly, 'it is the mischiefmak- ing driver trying to use up coal that he would otherwise have sold – he is worried about getting back to shed with more than usual in the tender'.

The picture I made with the blue XC and Bhadu Das had in the meantime been published. A search party was sent out at Bolpur to find him. He had grown considerably and was overjoyed with his picture. Bhadu was working out of town so one of his shoeshining friends was chosen for the companion picture to 'Cattle Boy', to be called 'Country Boy'. The scene was finally made on the last day of our epic week, depicting 'Country Boy' especially attired in red shorts sitting on a grassy embankment as the XC passed with the pickup freight. That evening we were to have a commemorative dinner at Bajpai's house, but on the run back from Bolpur we experienced delays in section and didn't reach Khana until 5pm. In order to be on time for dinner, it was decided that we should return to Burdwan by passenger train. Within minutes of getting down at Khana, the Rampurhat-to-Burdwan express came in behind a WP Pacific. Chaudhuri joined the train whilst Anupum, and I travelled footplate. 'Scrap iron', Anupum snapped, as he jabbed his finger towards the WP – the XCs were superior engines in every way. As we pulled out I moved over to the fireman's side to watch us overtake the XC.

Only one station lies between Khana Junction and Burdwan. I always cursed it for breaking up a potentially fast run down from the main line, but on this evening, Tallit, as the wayside halt is called, was to provide an experience I will never forget. As we ran in I saw that the XC had been held in the station. Our colour light flicked to green, but before we departed I noticed that No 22224 had received the right of way as well. The XC's chime whistle rang high above the WP's deeper tone as the two giants pulled out of the station side by side. It was sheer magic. Driver Sarkar was certainly going to challenge and issuing a throaty roar the XC quickly drew ahead of us. Our eleven-coach express hung heavy but Anupum grabbed the WP's regulator and opened it wide whilst the driver advanced the cut-off. The semi-streamliner responded with a forward lurch, but the XC had the scent of the chase, and to my sheer joy, remained ahead by several wagon lengths. The trails of smoke left by the two Pacifics as they did battle over the electrified main line were a spectacle within themselves. With maximum effort we inched our way past the XC's speeding wagons and drew alongside her. The two engines ran neck and neck, their crews exchanging shouts and waves. I was mesmerised by the sound of the XC at speed and the sight of her 6ft 2in-diameter driving wheels spinning gloriously. What an incredible way to end the British Pacific tradition – a tradition that began in 1908 when Churchward introduced his Great Bear and ended that afternoon in Bengal 73 years later with this last greyhound of British steam.

As speed increased, the roar from the two engines became deafening, until

'Country Boy' – the companion picture of Cattle Boy (see page 41) – this was made on the final heart rending day when this last greyhound of British steam was withdrawn from service. Anupam Banerjee is at the controls.

The team! Left to right: S. K. Sarker (driver); Sachin Roy (firing instructor); S. N. Bajpai (depot foreman); Colin Garratt, Maggie Grzyb, Santosh Chaudhuri (depot chargeman); S. Ansari (loco cleaner). On the footplate is T. P. Ghosh (fireman). Minutes later we put the Pacific in an inaccessible position behind the repair bay pending a preservation attempt.

after a couple of miles the XC was eased and soon disappeared in our smoke trail. Upon reaching Burdwan, Chaudhuri came up to the engine and explained that he had signalled driver Sarkar to refrain from any further thrills on account of No 22224's age and status.

An hour later, as we took our baths I heard the XC pass through the station en route to the shed. As her whistle died away the dynasty to which she belonged slipped into history and the terrible thunderstorm which broke over Burdwan that evening, and raged throughout our dinner, seemed eerily related to the event. Next morning the team assembled in front of No 22224 at Burdwan for a last farewell picture. I desperately wanted to preserve the engine and arranged with Bajpai not to dispatch her but to put her at the back of the shed behind the repair bay, thus making her inaccessible and providing time either for preservation in India or possible repatriation to Britain.

With deep sadness I once again left my friends at Burdwan and took the overnight express to Delhi, knowing as I went that a part of my life had died with that engine.

·12·

The Audio Visual Age

A talented copywriter from a Wardour Street advertising agency organised a glowing promotion on the new audio visual extravaganza we planned to launch. But I'd never seen an audio visual presentation in my life! I hadn't the foggiest idea how to produce the show, and had no one to help present it. Certainly not Stephanie, who was by now disenchanted with our lifestyle, its crises, economic restraints, and unsociable working hours. But committing myself in this way, was not so much irresponsibility as desperation – we had to improve our economy, or sink.

Help was needed desperately! I didn't have to look far, as in an adjacent cottage in Newton Harcourt – even closer to the childhood bridge than mine – lived an unemployed girl. Deciding to offer her the job we met in a local pub to discuss possibilities. I explained the need to produce a show to tour the country. I also explained that I could barely afford any wages. Prophetically it was St Valentine's Day!

With a launch date of 1 November, Maggie could hardly have understood what was being asked of her. A village girl, born and bred in Newton Harcourt, she was just nineteen years old; inexperienced; knew nothing about photography and had never heard of audio visual. That aside I couldn't believe anyone would last long at the pace and dedication which the organisation demanded and I gave Maggie a fortnight.

It was late spring before that lecture season ended, and no preparation had been done for the audio visual presentation. But already bookings had been made, the die was cast; there was no turning back. So we began to sift through my entire collection of transparencies, the fruits of twelve years' expeditions. Neglect throughout the seventies revealed that some pictures were in a sorry state, dampness in the cottage having caused colour deterioration. I had expected transparencies to last indefinitely, and was horrified to learn that the pictures could not be preserved on a long-term basis, due to regeneration. This discovery caused tremendous consternation, and threatened everything I had set out to achieve. We examined the definition of every picture through an X8 Agfa-lupe and those chosen were grouped into harmonious progressions for dissolving in AV sequences.

Maggie's devotion to the cause established a rapport between us, and we became inseparable. My marriage had become a predictable casualty of the horrendous pressures of work, and although Stephanie continued to live at the cottage for a time, the subsequent divorce dealt a hefty emotional and financial blow. So unstable were we financially, that there was every reason to abandon the AV project. But it was too late; Monica had received more bookings on fees which, even a year previously, would have been unimaginable.

We now had an idea of the picture sequences for a fast moving theatrical show. But how were we going to produce it? It was already July, and the launch date was less than four months away! My knowledge of AV programming was non-existent; I'd underestimated the phenomenal amount of professional attention needed. It seemed hopeless; the atmosphere at Newton Harcourt alternated erratically from abject depression to blind panic.

At the eleventh hour I learned that my friend and fellow railway author, Roger Crombleholme, had done some AV work, and since we could not afford a professional producer, I approached Roger with the crisis, and asked him to come and live at Newton Harcourt until the show was finished. He agreed. We converted the lounge into a studio, and along with local sound technician, John Williams, the four of us laboured day and night. For one week Roger didn't even leave the cottage! It was a painful process, but a script gradually took shape. Maggie did much of the pulsing, working with electronic feedback continuously buzzing in her ears. I can still see her ashen face as she sat, day after day, perfecting sequences to music. Just months after joining the organisation Maggie was showing prodigious mental energy and loyalty.

The countdown to the launch was plagued by a stream of appalling luck. Amplifiers went up in smoke and projectors spun crazily out of control. Equipment was changed, sold, or dumped as we struggled to find compatibility in an extremely sophisticated form of electronic technology.

By the second week in October, half the show was complete, although it was not in reliable working order. The pressure was increased by frenzied phone calls from Monica, demanding progress reports and assurances which a pale and exhausted Roger could not give. The cancellation of an AV show was drastically more serious than that of an ordinary club lecture, as Monica never failed to tell us. It left booked halls, printed tickets and audiences in mid-air. These anxieties weighed heavily.

We failed. The first ten bookings were cancelled and I substituted personal lectures leaving Maggie, Roger and John to complete the AV. Emotionally and physically exhausted, the last thing we wanted to face was an arduous season of bookings. There is a big difference between setting out to small clubs with a box of slides, and equipping, maintaining and manning a touring theatre show.

'In theatre'. Maggie at the business end of an Audio Visual bringing her innate abilities to bear as she prepares to change carousels in mid-flight.

The handbill from our ill-fated evening at Lewisham Concert Hall.

The cost of producing the AV had been so great that there was no hope of buying a suitable vehicle, yet the equipment would not fit into our Avenger saloon. We had to take heavy items out of their cases and wrap them in blankets; it was like the proverbial twenty students in a phone box! But the show proved a success. Audiences, albeit small at first, were fascinated by the new form of entertainment. It took time to develop a system to ensure equipment wasn't left behind. At one show we were greeted by a huge poster proclaiming 'Colin Garratt's AV Spectacular!' Whilst setting up Maggie's face turned white, and sidling up to me she whispered frantically, 'We've forgotten the projectors!' The case containing the projectors and pulsed tapes lay 160km away in Newton Harcourt. Our host whistled gaily as he uncoiled the speaker leads. Feeling an inch high, I explained our predicament. He stared at me in disbelief, as with an even reddening face said: 'But we expect 300 people!' From then on equipment was checked, and double-checked, right down to the soldering iron!

Our inexperience in a field of high technology rendered problems inevitable; equipment failures were endemic. We needed a proper servicing backup, but finances forbade this. At Lewisham Concert Hall, we turned up to the awesome sight of my name circling the building in lights. 'We've arrived!' I thought, 'here is just reward for all the years of hard work and dedication.' The triumph was short lived; hardly had the show started when the proverbial chickens hatched! The tape began to run slow, my voice grinding painfully deeper and more distorted. Maggie's pleas of 'Do something!' were ignored as I waited for the problem to go away. It didn't. Maggie was so embarrassed that she threatened to lock herself in the Ladies. This forced me into action; I ran from the balcony, down the back stairway, across the foyer, through the stalls and up onto the stage, in order to tell the audience what was already self-evident. The manager, soon on the scene, was suitably distressed and as I arranged to do a personal lecture he announced a premature interval, leaving the entire audience to file out to the bar.

But we were popular and as bookings increased, we found ourselves living a 'life on the road'. Travelling the country on one-night stands is glamorous but punishing. Waiting behind a stage curtain, for clearance to go on, is a moment when few people – no matter how professional – can avoid nerves; it is not easy to walk into a dazzling spotlight knowing that in the blackness before you several hundred people are hanging onto your every word. But once the lights are down, it's all up to the projectionist. For two hours Maggie has to be constantly aware; checking focussing, registration, sound level, and changing trays to split-second timing. Maggie is responsible if anything goes wrong. Sitting alone in a darkened hall, with the enjoyment of several hundred people at her fingertips, is a daunting task.

It was a gruelling schedule; we would leave Newton around midday and be

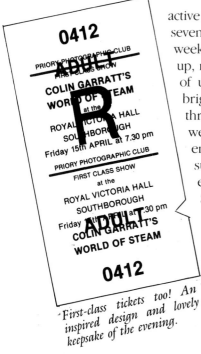

First-class tickets too! An inspired design and lovely keepsake of the evening.

active until the early hours of the following morning – six or seven days a week! This meant up to forty hours' driving a week for me, and constant loading, unloading and setting-up, not to mention performing the show! The succession of unrelenting one-night stands became a way of life; bright lights, filled theatres and long black journeys through the night. It demanded superhuman energy and we remained permanently hyped-up, depending entirely on the electrical feedback from audiences to sustain us. We learnt to relax on the motorways in the early hours, running deep into the night alongside the Sainsbury's, Tesco and Securicor vans; but we were never more than a hair's breadth from total exhaustion. Only by playing dates nationwide, night after night, could we hope to fund the all-important global expeditions.

During the second season we attracted the attention of BBC television producers who wanted to do an Omnibus documentary on my life and work. They came to Newton Harcourt to discuss the film and were fascinated by the village, with my childhood bridge, and it was with that that they opened the programme. I had hoped that the BBC would whisk us away to some foreign location, but the Omnibus budget didn't run that far and we had to find a theme in Britain. I chose the combination of steam and coal – lifeblood of the Industrial Revolution – and we filmed at Cadley Hill – the last British colliery using steam traction. The climax of the Omnibus film was to be Maggie and I doing a show in front of a specially-invited BBC audience at Ealing Town Hall.

It was like a Royal Premiere; my parents came from Norfolk, Monica arrived – clad in furs, Terry Hill was there from Praktica, along with representatives from Agfa Gevaert. We were stars for the night! At 7.30 the cameras rolled. Then it happened – the equipment went berserk! One of the projectors began to jump pulses, the pictures went out of phase, the music out of time, and my commentary out of synch. 'Why now?' 'Why, why, why?' We stopped and started a dozen times, but it was useless. The BBC technicians were unperturbed; they had captured what they wanted – myself in front of the audience, the projectors lighting up, and Maggie working the equipment. But the specially-invited audience never did see the show!

Despite the breakdowns, demand for our shows increased and all seemed set fair when to our horror we lost Praktica. It was ironic that after being supported for so long playing small clubs, our progression to national theatre coincided with the loss of their support.

The cottage was turned into a TV studio during the making of the BBC's Omnibus *documentary. Peter Bartlett – with back to camera – is directing.* (Leicester Mercury)

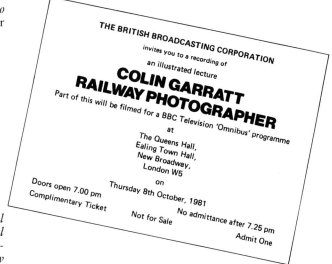

THE BRITISH BROADCASTING CORPORATION

invites you to a recording of

an illustrated lecture

COLIN GARRATT
RAILWAY PHOTOGRAPHER

Part of this will be filmed for a BBC Television 'Omnibus' programme

at

The Queens Hall,
Ealing Town Hall,
New Broadway,
London W5

on

Thursday 8th October, 1981

Doors open 7.00 pm

Complimentary Ticket

No admittance after 7.25 pm

Not for Sale

Admit One

The holders of the BBC's special invites for our Audio Visual evening for the Omnibus *programme were treated to a floorshow they hadn't expected!*

Fortunately the years of playing the clubs had established a reputation good enough to convince David King, the Exhibition and Promotions Manager of Canon Cameras, to adopt us. He offered logistical support, and I switched to the Canon system. Having spent ten years using the cheapest reflex camera, I now had the privilege of working with the Canon F1, the flagship of their range and the finest 35mm camera available. With the Canon lenses came infinitely sharper pictures that not only revolutionised what our audiences saw on the screen, but greatly improved the quality of colour plates in my books.

David King became a close friend and mentor, and we in turn had to do our best for Canon. A show bearing the Agfa and Canon logos suggested professional entertainment and having amplifiers going up in smoke or pictures going out of synch, was simply not on. These problems were finally resolved by David Kerr, the entrepreneurial Sales Manager of Electrosonic of Woolwich. David was interested in working with us on a new production and took us out of our country cottage and into Electrosonic's studio. Here we formulated the second show, *Colin Garratt's Great Railway Adventure* which, thanks to the reliability of Electrosonic's equipment, played to happy audiences for two seasons. The light at the end of the tunnel was becoming brighter, and with Electrosonic's continued assistance, production began on a third AV spectacular, which included music specially written and recorded by composer Michael Jacques. Called *Round the World in Search of Steam*, it continues to play successfully to this day. Agfa took a keen interest in these shows as vital support from Philip Miller, Agfa's head of Corporate Relations, had to be justified in hard marketing terms.

But our fourth theatre show – currently in production – will be the 'pièce de résistance'! It is being produced by Peter Sarner Audio Visual & Television of Shepherd's Bush, Britain's leading communications facility house and a company with an endless list of successful productions. The privilege of using Sarner's expertise and advanced production facilities is another milestone in taking railways to people and – at long last – will vindicate every superlative used by my imaginative friend from Wardour Street.

·13·
The Broad Gauge Discovery

One would imagine the tiny mid-Atlantic islands of the Azores as the last place on earth to have a 7ft-gauge railway, and yet for years rumours persisted about two broad gauge locomotives existing there. The Azores were not known to have ever had railways and the islands were so small that a 2ft 6in gauge would have been more likely. The story remained nothing more than a fanciful notion until I received this letter in 1976, following an article I'd written for *Weekend* magazine.

Rua da Conceição, 14
S Vincente Ferreira,
St Michael's, Azores

The Editor, WEEKEND
  Northcliffe House
    London EC4Y 0JA

18 November 1976

Dear Sir,

GHOSTS ON THE LINE

    This is the title across pages 20–21 of No 3738 of WEEKEND for 20–26 October 1976, and the story under it is really interesting.

    Mr and Mrs Garratt would perhaps like to know that the Port Authority, Ponta Delgada, St Michael's, The Azores Islands, own and operate one of those ghosts – a very old steam locomotive, 50hp, 60 tons pull, which since the last quarter of last century has played an important part in constructing, lengthening, up-keeping the wharf and the breakwater at this Island.

    Would you please pass the news on to the Garratt team?

    Thanking you in anticipation, I am, dear Sir,

Yours faithfully,

(Mr) Laudalino de Melo Ponte

So the Azores did have a railway. But what was the gauge? Our subsequent letter to Sn Ponte remained unanswered. Not having the finances to travel out to the Azores and solve the mystery, the idea continued to haunt me until, in

1981, I commissioned a Portuguese interpreter to come to Newton Harcourt and sit by the phone until the matter was resolved.

It took several hours to obtain the telephone number of the harbour at Ponta Delgada, but finally we made contact with the harbour master himself, who was questioned on the existence of a railway. Breathlessly I waited; the flurry of Portuguese seemed to go on for ever. Eventually, turning aside from the phone, my interpreter confirmed that a railway was there but had not been used in many years and only two locomotives remained. 'Ask him what the gauge is!' I replied immediately. The answer came. 'He doesn't know'. 'Right then', I announced, grasping the poor woman's arm, 'ask him to send somebody out to measure the distance between the rails, and we will call again in an hour'.

After some confusion, agreement was reached and we sat over pots of tea in the cottage in suspended animation. Visions of Brunel's dream, an exotic expedition, the only broad gaugers left in the world, all flooded through my mind. We booked our call which, in the event, took two hours to come through. Again a frenzied conversation in Portuguese whilst I sat in anticipation until the interpreter announced, 'The harbour master has sent a runner to measure the width but the rails are buried in the soil and he cannot find them'. 'Listen', I said in desperation, 'this is extremely important. Ask him to send a runner to dig out the rails and measure them. Tell him that I'm an historian, tell him I'm writing a book; tell him anything!' We were asked to ring back at two o'clock the following afternoon; I was a nervous wreck, but at least the harbour master was being co-operative. With the interpreter reinstated in the cottage, we rang at the appointed time. The harbour master was not in his office and no one knew anything about our quest, 'Ring back at four o'clock', we were told. We did and contacted directly with the harbour master. 'The distance between the rails is 213cm', he declared. The conversion had already been done, exactly 7ft. Unbelievable! The dream had come true. So overjoyed was I that I asked the harbour master to book me into an hotel, for I would arrive on the island at the end of that week. At ten the following day I phoned my bank and the money for the expedition was guaranteed.

In the early hours of a damp November morning five days later I left Newton Harcourt bound for Lisbon, and finally arrived at Ponta Delgada on the island of São Miguel at eight o'clock the same evening. Despite the long journey I was eager to go out and search the harbour that night but restrained my ardour and fell into a restless sleep. Upon waking the next morning I opened my window to a sunny, blustery day with the sky covered in enormous white clouds, and the purest air I had ever experienced. My sense of well being was heightened by the arrival of a guide assigned by the harbour master to escort me to the engines. His name was Alvaro Saraiva and, to my delight, spoke excellent English. He was a little younger than myself and oozed energy; we took an immediate liking to one another. 'Do you like girls?' he asked, as we drove

Notice the width of the Black Hawthorn's buffer beam and the distance between the rails and visualise a whole new concept, a whole lost potential for railways.

through the town. 'Yes, I like girls', I replied. 'Are you married?' 'No, not married, but I live with someone'. 'Is she beautiful?' 'Yes', I said, 'she's very beautiful'. 'In the Azores', Alvaro confided, 'we have many beautiful girls'. 'But I have come here for locomotives', I said seriously.

Soon we arrived at the old dock area at the far end of the harbour. It was now little more than a junk yard, with derelict harbour machinery and old, upturned boats. 'There they are', Alvaro shouted as he stopped the vehicle. I could see nothing, until a rusty chimney top protruding above a mass of debris caught my attention. Peering through the junk, a whole new dimension of railways opened up as I perceived the breathtaking beauty of a 7ft-gauge locomotive, the sheer monumentality of Brunel's vision; for this apparition made the standard gauge look like a toy. Photography, however, was impossible as there was so much harbour debris around that the second engine was completely covered. I explained the difficulty to Alvaro who disappeared to discuss the problem with the harbour authorities. He returned beaming 'Come on', he said, 'let's go and have lunch, as afterwards I have organised a crane, a heavy-duty forklift truck, a lorry and six men, to clear the site'. We worked feverishly that afternoon and the next day, by which time the second engine stood clear. As I surveyed the two giants, I became aware of the strange irony of my having travelled thousands of miles to these semi-tropical islands only to find that the first locomotive was from Leicestershire, the Falcon Works at Loughborough, about thirty kilometres from the cottage, while the second one to be uncovered hailed from Black Hawthorn in Gateshead in 1883.

Unfortunately, the engines had been placed buffer to buffer and my next task was to separate them to give the picture proper dimension. I put this problem to Alvaro who went off in search of the harbour master whilst I took a spade and began to dig out the rails from under the soil. He returned two hours later, riding atop the most hideous pneumatic forklift truck and beaming all over his face. Lashings of steel coil were applied to the Falcon's frames and the forklift, revved to screaming pitch, was flung into gear, and in a subsequent violent cataclysm of movement lurched the locomotive forward very slightly. I had actually seen a broad gauge move; again and again came the violent antics of the forklift until, bit by bit, the engines were sufficiently separated.

Our activities in the harbour scrapyard quickly attracted the attention of the media. Azores television arrived, along with a journalist from the island's newspaper. None of them knew of the locomotives' significance. I told them of the 'Battle of the Gauges' and Brunel – 'Who is he?' they asked. I mentioned the Industrial Revolution – 'We didn't have it', they replied. So the story was of tremendous interest to them, not least as the majority of their viewers had never seen a train, and few even knew of their own railway. The harbour workers, however, remained bemused as to why an Englishman should come so far and conduct such bizarre activities for the sake of two old engines which didn't even work. Any credibility I had in their eyes was lost when I decided that the engines needed brightening up for photography.

I accompanied Alvaro to market to buy a weak red paint which I believed would provide a suitable contrast and Alvaro contentedly set about applying it to various parts of the Falcon. We were surrounded by spectators. Their faces showing complete incomprehension that the lunatic was being aided and abetted by one of their own countrymen. Surveying Alvaro's work, I soon realised that my 'weak red' was actually looking gaudy, it was too strong and needed toning down to suit the derelict atmosphere, so I then threw clods of damp soil at the parts Alvaro had painted. This played down the colour perfectly yet retained the contrast. The crowd could not believe their eyes, their comments which Alvaro humorously interpreted revealed utter incredulity that one man should paint while the other threw mud.

One major obstacle only remained before successful photography could begin – how to remove the hideous white wall which loomed behind the engines. 'Well, we can't knock that down', Alvaro said, reading my expression. 'Then what can we cover it with?' I asked. There was nothing. 'Could we cover it with branches?' I asked. Alvaro shrugged. 'We have no trees on the coastline, only in the interior of the island and then on private estates', he said. But trees were the only solution, so next morning Alvaro turned up at the hotel in a large harbour authority lorry with two burly man-handlers sitting in the back with axes. We roared out of the town heading for the interior of the island.

Soon the open truck was piled high with tall, young conifers, and we made our way back to the harbour, and deposited them in an enormous pile next to the Falcon. Assembly began after lunch; it was a daunting task. The wall was twenty-four metres long and the conifers were as heavy as mahogany, and with no soft ground to lodge them in, placement was extremely difficult. We

After we had reset the conifers I made this scene of the broad gaugers being lashed by a squally storm.

laboured for several hours, finally managing to cover the wall, but no sooner had we stood back to admire our work than the sky darkened and the wind began to rise. A squally mid-Atlantic storm was on its way. Twenty minutes later the storm struck and the mighty gusts of wind felled the line of conifers one by one and even blew some of the smaller ones away up the harbour. Alvaro turned to me, looking as if he wished I'd go home.

The storm was brief and by six o'clock radiant sunshine had returned. But the volatile mid-Atlantic climate meant that free-standing conifers were useless and Alvaro promised to locate some coils of heavy duty wire. The whole of the next morning was taken up replacing and lashing the trees into place, a job which Alvaro conducted with tremendous ingenuity and by lunchtime the trees were invincible against any tempest. There now followed two days of blissful photography, the mid-Atlantic climate ranged from fabulous cloud effects – the hangover from spent storms – to crystal clear light and ferocious gusty squalls. All of which enabled the rusted hulks to be depicted in a variety of moods by day and night.

Having completed my photography I was received by the Governor of the Azores to put the case for preservation of both engines with the possible option of one being repatriated to Britain. He assured me that everyone in the Azores now knew the significance of the relics and that they would not be broken up.

Back in England, widespread national publicity was given; an interview on BBC Radio 4's 'Today' programme, a full colour page in the *Illustrated London News* and four pages in Mike George's *Steam Railway Magazine*.

I was approached by many people to co-ordinate a campaign for preservation and actually received an offer of free shipping. Unhappily, the best I could do (as in so many other cases) was to draw national attention to the situation. Not so much as a phone call or a word of interest or encouragement came from the National Railway Museum in York – the organisation responsible for the preservation of Britain's railway heritage.

Although nothing could be done to return one of these priceless relics to Britain, I later received a letter from the Governor of the Azores, saying that both engines had now been taken from the scrapyard. One had been placed in the museum at Ponta Delgada and the other was being displayed in the university gardens.

At least they had been preserved and at least I had depicted two locomotives which represent all that's left of one of the most illuminating flashes of genius to emanate from the nineteenth century. If, today, we had that network of 7ft-gauge main lines, instead of a network of motorways, Britain would be a happier, healthier and more prosperous nation in which to live. The last of that great dream and vision fizzled out in a harbour scrapyard lashed by squally storms in the middle of the Atlantic Ocean.

·14·
Sudan – a Saloon of our Own

Our expedition to the Sudan was to experience a superb British railway whose main line from north to south was almost 2,200km long. Maggie and I arrived in Khartoum shortly before Christmas in 1982, and the Under Secretary of State for Transport, Brigadier Hassan El Amin Salih, warmly welcomed us. We were allocated an inspection saloon in which to live as we toured the system. Complete with cook/attendant, the saloon would be attached to the service trains as required and set off in sidings whilst our work was done. The brigadier also arranged a guide – Mustafa Karrar, from the Ministry of Culture.

Boxing Day was spent shopping for supplies. That evening a railway vehicle collected us from the hotel and drove us to the goods yard. After bumping over a dozen sidings the driver proceeded between lines of wagons until the head-lamps picked out a handsome cream bogie saloon. The door opened and our attendant gazed down upon his guests. 'Meet Hussin', Karrar said as we surveyed a small, dark benign-looking Nubian. Hussin knew no English, but seemed delighted to be with us. The furnishings and fittings were magnificent, harking back to a time when Sudan's railways were in their prime. There was a lounge/dining room, double bedroom, bathroom, attendant's sleeping quarters, and kitchen. It was carpeted throughout, was roomy and had space allocated for bicycles, for us to use on short-haul journeys when encamped. I thought of the inspection saloon containing trilby-hatted officials that had frightened me so much as a child. Never did I dream that one day, over thirty years later, I would reside in one.

Soon the whine of an English Electric diesel could be heard in the yards, and our vehicle was attached to a northbound empty stock train. We heard the rumble of the girder bridge over the Blue Nile as we headed off into the night, bound for the legendary railway town of Atbara.

The saloon was well sprung, and the beds so comfortable that, despite the rough track, we slept soundly. When we awoke the sun was already high and the landscape a golden desert, punctuated by isolated villages. A film of dust had settled in the saloon, changing the form of objects as if they had been sprinkled with a light fall of snow. Hussin appeared with breakfast; 'foulmasri' (beans in sauce) with lashings of bread and a pot of orange marmalade.

The train arrived in Atbara at midday and we transferred to the railway guest

Our team and saloon left to right: CG, Hashim Osman, Mustafa Karrar, Hussin and Maggie.

house, and were given a superb double room with a balcony. Lunch was served with Sheffield cutlery and Staffordshire crockery, marked 'Sudan Railways'; the coffee pots being Sheffield plate from Mappin & Webb. Heinz ketchup completed the scene!

Once Africa's second most industrialised town, Atbara was disturbingly quiet. The works contained dozens of derelict and partly dismantled engines, steam and diesel. There was an astonishing variety of types including North British 4-8-2s, Mikados and Pacifics, whilst the works' pilot was a Hunslet 0-6-0T built in 1950 – one of the last main line 0-6-0 shunting tanks in the world. It provided a remarkable contrast with an 0-6-0 diesel mechanical built by Hawthorn Leslie/ English Electric in 1936, reminding us that dieselisation of Sudan Railways began half a century previously and was still by no means complete!

Every nut and bolt of that incredible works had come from Britain and so absorbed were we in all the machinery, plant and rolling stock, that it was twilight before we left. The drive back to the guest house was through tree-lined avenues, set out by the British in what was once an upper-class residential area for railway officials. A ferry had crossed the river from the opposite bank and donkey carts, goats, and colourful gaggles of women bringing their produce to Atbara market could be seen silhouetted against one of the unforgettable sunsets of the Nile. After dinner, coffee and cigars were enjoyed on the terrace. The lush vegetation around assumed the sounds of a tropical night; we could have been in the colonial period of half a century before.

Next morning we went to see the works manager, who had been trained at Doncaster during the early sixties, and heard in detail the tragedy that had befallen Sudan Railways. He explained how every conceivable engine had been cannibalised for spares to keep a handful of engines in service. 'What shall I do when the next lot come for shopping?' he asked. 'Shall I jump into the Nile?' The reality was all too apparent – the railway was on the brink of shutdown.

We talked to his colleagues, most of whom had been trained at BR establishments. Their problems were legion. The railway was being forced to apply ridiculous tariffs in order to keep prices low and exports cheap. The government sometimes ordered goods be carried free of charge, even from industries that could afford to pay. Lack of foreign exchange prevented the purchase of essential spares for locomotives and rolling stock. It was also stated that the exchange which Sudan did earn was often wasted on lavish items for government officials – perks such as Mercedes cars. The decline caused many fine railwaymen to abandon the service and hardly any middle management was left, whilst top management carried the can for ministerial incompetence. The workforce was grossly oversized but government had forbidden any reduction for fear of union action. Inevitably wages were low, resulting in a lack of staff discipline. Also it had become difficult to get workers to base themselves in the outstations where conditions are Spartan.

The complexity of maintaining diesels had also become a headache and it was clear to me that buying them wasted precious exchange, which should have been spent on track, rolling stock and signalling. Vast sections of permanent way needed renovation; speeds were little better than a crawl and derailments frequent. What conceivable advantage is there in running complex diesel-electrics over such a railway?

Saudi Arabia and Germany have given vast amounts of money but for building roads! Trucks and cars have flooded the country, so weakening the railway further. Maggie and I shared feelings of frustration and anger that this vast enterprise built and run by Britain over so many years, should be allowed to go to rack and ruin to the detriment of Sudan.

The parts for which they were desperate at Atbara were straightforward in terms of British technology – steel tyres, injectors, tubes, super-heaters, fireboxes and tube-plates – yet these simple items could not be obtained. It was a sorry and totally unnecessary state of affairs.

After a week in Atbara, the saloon was attached to a southbound passenger train back to Khartoum. Here I had a meeting with the General Manager of

*Manufacturing spares at Atbara Works. Many items can be made here but some parts –
though simple technology to the west – are beyond Sudan's capacity and the railway virtually
ground to a halt for want of them.*

Sudan Railways, Mohammed Abdel Rahan Wasfi to propose a railway museum.
Small recompense for the devastation witnessed at Atbara. He confirmed
support, agreeing with my sentiments that it should be an Anglo-Sudanese
project, including the possibility of repatriation of certain items to Britain. We
drew up a list of feasible items before continuing on the next leg of our
adventure.

Two days later with a decrepit English Electric diesel at our head – which
looked unnervingly like a Peak – we rumbled southwards, accompanied by
Hashim Osman, Karrar having temporarily returned to the ministry. Our
destination was Sennar Junction, the best steam centre in Sudan.

During the journey we passed through the Gezira Project, a vast cotton and
agricultural scheme initiated by the British in the twenties. Gaily coloured
women could be seen picking cotton, and moving across the hard earth, with
the dignity of the gleaners in Millet's famous painting.

Sennar was reached in the early hours, and after some bumpy shunting the saloon was deposited in a siding next to the shed yard; all around was the sound of locomotives. Ten were in service; seven Pacifics and three Mikados. Dominating the depot yard was a stationary boiler complete with huge extending chimney. I've always been fascinated by stationary boilers, and this one reminded me of childhood fears, particularly when the operator was up on the platform attending to the injectors and silhouetted as though he were the driver of some ethereal dreamlike monster. The boiler became a priority at Sennar, but in order to capture its surreal atmosphere, I needed one of Sudan's celebrated sunsets. Every evening around four o'clock, we would watch the sky and ask Hussin's advice as to whether he thought a sunset would form.

Life at Sennar was pleasant. There was a good market, and Hussin found all sorts of unexpected goodies, including Heinz beans and a huge packet of Kellogg's Corn Flakes. Where he unearthed them, we'll never know. He used to come back clutching an exotic find, beaming all over his face, knowing that the purchase would meet with our approval. It was fascinating to see our friends at the depot decked in their greasy overalls until two o'clock, and then see them an hour later passing along the railway in their robes and turbans on the way to the mosque. One particular delight at Sennar was the vast flocks of yellow wagtails that passed over in the early evening. Many of these were Europe's wintering flocks, attracted by the presence of the nearby Sennar Dam.

One afternoon, as Maggie and I were working in the shed, Hussin appeared, pointing to the sky. A wash of light cloud had weakened the usual blue colour – tonight would be a 'sunset night'. We returned to the saloon, collected our lighting equipment, and proceeded to set up the cameras and lights around the stationary boiler. We watched the sunset mature, and when it reached a beautiful crescendo, we let fly the flash units to capture one of the most successful pictures of the tour, a picture which oozed all the childhood fear these awesome apparitions had evoked.

Photography was excellent in Sennar, and six happy days were spent there before Hashim arranged for the saloon to be attached to the twice weekly passenger train from Khartoum to El Damazeen, close to the Ethiopian border. The ten-coach train steamed away in fine style behind one of Sennar's blue Pacifics.

The principal stop on the 217km journey was at Singa where the train was besieged by local traders selling drinks and food to the passengers. The station master took us to his office for tea, and as we sat, he passed me a Ladybird book of locomotives translated into Arabic. It was my book! When the station master realised I was the author, he produced his young son – to whom the book belonged – to shake hands with me.

Our priority in El Damazeen was to see the Clayton steam railcar that was dumped there. Our engine's squeaky LNER-type whistle rang boldly as we

The steam railcar was the ancestor of today's diesel units and the example at Damazeen is one of the last on earth. Notice the water-filler at the front end.

approached and there, glowing under the arc lamps of the shed yard, stood the Clayton. What a discovery! Damazeen's superintendent was on the platform to greet us, and, after shaking hands, we hustled him off to the railcar, telling him what an important relic it was – a perfect exhibit for the museum. 'She's built like a battleship,' I said to Maggie as I climbed into the cab. But the words died on my lips, for an open space confronted me – the vertical boiler and valve gear were missing! With heavy hearts we continued to explore the rusted ghost. It was almost identical to the eleven steam railcars built by Clayton Wagons for the LNER between 1927 and 1928. These commemorated famous stage coaches and bore such exciting names as *Chevy Chase, Bang Up, Comet* and *Rapid.*

Upon return to the saloon, Hussin had our tray of pre-dinner coffee ready. No sooner had we sat down than there came an almighty bang and the coffee was sent flying through the air. We had been the victim of a heavy shunting movement; coffee, sugar and biscuits were everywhere. Our papers were soaked, the cameras were wet and Hussin, cursing passionately in Arabic, proceeded on all fours to clear up the mess with the aid of a bucket and cloth. It was midnight before we finally got to sleep, but not for long. At one o'clock I heard a train arrive from Sennar and when the engine came on shed it was berthed alongside our saloon. The noise was deafening; not only was she leaking badly in several places, but the steam supply to the dynamo had been left on, causing an unrelenting high-pitched whistle. I knew what was going to happen. Sure enough, within minutes a loud thump was heard. The kitchen door was flung open and Hussin remonstrated violently into the darkness of the shed yard. Whatever excuses were given, they only made him more furious and his abuse rated amongst the best I have ever heard. After a vindictive and grossly overprolonged roar from the cylinder cocks – obviously intended to annoy Hussin – the offending engine was moved out of earshot. Long after it had gone, Hussin's cursings and mumblings were audible throughout the saloon.

Our final location was Kosti and having returned to Sennar we continued southwards down the main line. The journey took two days and as we headed southwards the country became increasingly wild; massive termite mounds appeared on the trackside and camels freely roamed amid a golden landscape studded with baobab trees. Kosti is an important transhipment point between the railway and the Nile for goods going to Malakal and Juba in the deep south. The railway continues westwards from Kosti to Nyala and Wau. Nyala was soon to be in the eye of the world due to the severe famines in the Darfur region.

Kosti is noted for its 500 class 4-8-2s and, having arrived during the night, I was awakened by the combined sounds of Hussin preparing breakfast and the heavy exhaust beats of an engine shunting. Lifting the bedroom curtain, I noticed a blue rock thrush standing on a mound of earth, whilst several tracks away protruding above a line of wagons was a gleaming blue 500 class. What a sight! 'Maggie, Maggie!' I cried, 'blue rock thrush and blue 500!' But by the time she had woken up the bird had flown away and the 500 had disappeared from sight, although its throaty cough continued to reverberate around the yards.

The 500 left later that morning with a freight for El Obeid, leaving the only other example in steam on shed. She was booked next day to run light-engine to Knana cement factory. The journey to Knana involves crossing the Nile Swing Bridge north of Kosti before running along the main line to Rabak, the junction for the Knana branch. Hashim arranged for our saloon to go with the engine and as the 500 always stopped to shunt at Rabak, it was decided that Maggie and I would go ahead to prepare our photographic locations. We were especially interested in the derailed 500 class engine on its side on the Knana line.

Next morning the engine collected our saloon, and we bowled away north-wards in fine style, the coach swaying and buffeting to every lurch of the locomotive. As we roared over the Nile bridge at 80km/h, poor old Hussin sat on the kitchen floor desperately holding the kettle in place on the stove in order to serve our morning coffee before work began.

The track trolley was waiting for us at Rabak and we set off along the branch. Five kilometres down we found the wreck; it was very derelict and had been

The struggle to keep the huge 500 Class in service was unremitting. Now, thanks to Band Aid, some of these engines have been fully overhauled.

partly cannibalised. Having selected the right focal length and viewpoint we arranged several 'run pasts' of our gleaming blue engine passing its fallen sister. It was as dramatic a way of putting the 500s on film as I could have wished.

We spent several days at Kosti working with the 500s. As recently as 1955, forty-two of these powerful engines were delivered from North British. Now for want of simple spares, forty of them were lying idle.

Our programme over, we returned to Khartoum. Our saloon was berthed in the goods yard and we remained there until our return to England. I had learnt a lot and seen, once again, the tragedy that can befall a once great railway. There was undoubtedly a place for Britain in an ongoing relationship with the systems she formerly owned. Indeed, there was a role for the whole railway community in Britain, and the need for a museum to preserve this particular Anglo-Sudanese heritage.

With these thoughts in mind, I had a meeting with the Minister of Transport. He reiterated the need for help, asking that when we returned to Britain, we publicised the situation in the hope that a greater liaison could be forged between the two countries. I promised him that we would do everything in our power for the cause of railways.

At sunset, we went up to the station to make a last gorgeous silhouette picture of the signal boxes, track layout and semaphores – we could have been in Wellingborough! Our last day in Sudan was spent with journalists from *Sudanow Magazine* which published an article on our reactions to all we had seen, and that night Hussin's cooking excelled itself at a farewell dinner arranged in the saloon with Mustafa Karrar and Hashim.

At four in the morning a car arrived to take us to the airport. Hussin stood watching from the doorway, waving sadly. He still didn't know a word of English, nor we Arabic, yet we had enjoyed one another's company throughout and fervently hoped that there would be another time.

Within twenty-four hours of arriving home, I received a phone call from Granada TV. The Serpell report had just been published – would I go to Liverpool to participate in a live debate on railways? The newspapers were full of Serpell. That a group of men could run up a bill of three-quarters of a million pounds for producing such tripe was frightening, and I realised that Sudan's railways were really no more threatened than our own. At least in Sudan there existed a national will to rehabilitate the railways, whereas clearly only destructive forces were at work in Britain. The fight for railways had to come nationally and internationally, Sudanese and British railways representing two sides of the same coin.

'A tale of two engines'. Our resplendent 500 Class approaches a sister engine lying on its side like the carcass of a huge animal. Our saloon is visible in the approaching train.

·15·

Adventures Behind the Iron Curtain

Sinister arc lights illuminated the minefields of no man's land. Endless security guards, dogs and barbed wire characterised the forbidding nature of the East German border. A probing search of our motor caravan ensued; wires were dropped into the petrol tank, trolleys with mirrors pushed beneath the vehicle, and every item from inside examined in detail. There was one defect. Maggie had brought a book of UFOs for reading on the tour – forbidden literature! A higher official was summoned to examine it. After careful deliberation he threw it moodily back into the bunk. It was midnight before we reached the Polish border at Gorlitz; the roads were poorly lit, badly signposted, and we were exhausted. But Maggie (her name is Grzyb), whose father had come to Britain from Poland after World War II, was back in her homeland. Somehow it was irresistibly tranquil. The West, with all its glittering merchandise and freedom, seemed but a fantasy.

Railway photography being ostensibly forbidden in Poland, it was one of those countries I'd always 'kept on ice'. I finally saw a way to get in when the BBC produced a book on their 'Great Little Railways' series, for which I had done 'The Dragons of Sugar Island', and I was invited to contribute a chapter on this film. The series had been heavily criticised for lack of railway content, in particular the film on Poland. So Sheila Abelman of BBC Publications requested that I go to Poland under their auspices to obtain relevant material for the book. The Director General himself signed the letter that requested we be given full facilities by the Polish authorities. This was sent to Warsaw via the Foreign Office, and in May 1983 Maggie and I set off for Poland.

On arrival in Warsaw we received papers enabling us to cover specified areas. The most significant aspect of our work for the BBC was the narrow gauge line between Znin and Gasawa. This serves the railway museum in Wenecja, as well as the reconstructed Lusatian Fort at Biskupin. At the railway museum we met Leon Lichocinski, a sprightly seventy-seven-year-old who, dressed in full station master's uniform, acted as museum guide. A great showman, he would lead his audience to an engine, climb into the cab and address visitors like a preacher in a pulpit.

One of the engines in the museum was the predecessor of the historic Feldbahns, the German military engines of World War I. We learnt from Leon

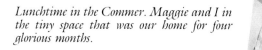

Lunchtime in the Commer. Maggie and I in the tiny space that was our home for four glorious months.

Maggie in the Feldbahn grave-yard at Czarna Bialostocka. Notice the diminutive size of these war veterans – the Feld-bahn tipping the scales in full working order at only 12½ tons.

that survivors existed in the primeval woodlands of Baliostok, in the north-east, close to the Russian border. I had assumed the Feldbahns to be extinct, but so important was this information we decided to make the journey up to the forests knowing the Feldbahns would be an exciting addition to the BBC's story. Upon returning to Warsaw the ministry issued our credentials and we were given a letter of introduction to the Baliostok forestry authorities.

It was a five-hour drive to Baliostok and the only person who spoke English was the conservation officer, Krzystof Wolfram. After giving us an account of the flora and fauna in the area, he came to the matter in hand; 'Feldbahns? Yes, they came here after the World War I. Maybe there are some remaining at Czarna – I will take you there'.

But at Czarna all we found was the Feldbahns' graveyard; ten of them lying in an overgrown dump – the only active engines being new diesels from Karl Marx city. Moodily Maggie and I examined the hulks, Krzystof took our letter to the authorities. He returned an hour later smiling and gesticulating; 'One of them's still working! It's coming in with a train!' Within the hour, magnificent plumes of steam announced the arrival of Feldbahn TX No 1117 – built by Henschel of Kassel in 1918 – with a very long train. She was the last survivor, and would soon be withdrawn. We drove the Commer into the graveyard, where we lived for several days whilst photographing No 1117 and her moribund sisters until our visas ran out forcing us to return to Warsaw. We were unsure of our position; would we be evicted from Poland? Would the secret police suddenly pounce saying we had no right to have gone to the forest, and confiscate our films? With the BBC work done there was no reason for the authorities to allow us to stay, but after ten difficult days of negotiations we were called to the Ministry of Transport and asked exactly what we wanted to do.

I had my heart set on the Kamieniec-to-Klodsko section of the international main line from Wroclaw to Prague. This line carried sixteen steam passenger trains a day worked by the magnificent Pt 47 express Mikados – classic locomotives with huge windshields and a 1930s appearance; we asked if we could be allowed to remain by the lineside for three weeks making pictures. Amazingly, permission was granted, and with a three-week extension stamped in our passports, we left Warsaw and headed south-west towards Silesia.

Kamieniec is a small market town, and we found a superb cutting, in glorious countryside, a mile from the station where a bridge carrying a cart track crossed the railway. We decided to make this bridge our home.

Our first task was to register with the local police, and to inform them that we were living up at the bridge and had the blessing of the ministry. I felt it would be helpful if we found someone who spoke English. We scoured Kamieniec, asking in very stunted Polish, 'Do you speak English?' only to be met with blank incomprehension. We were on the point of giving up when a man motioned us to follow him to a large house set back from the road. Indicating the second floor, he said 'Dabrowska'. In we went, up the stone staircase to the second floor and banged on the door of the nearest apartment. An old lady answered. 'Dabrowska', we said and she immediately pointed to the door opposite. Another lady answered and we repeated the magic word. In a chatter of Polish she invited us in and called her daughter who was studying English at college, the only person in Kamieniec who knew our language. Her name was Eva and we took an immediate liking to her, but so surprised was she at being confronted by two English people – the first she'd ever met – that she completely clammed up and forgot everything she'd learnt. It took her two hours to thaw out and put her remarkably good English into use. 'We will go to the police, but after that you will not cook dinner in your caravan, you will eat with us!'

The Dabrowskas made us very welcome and the summer days melted into one another as we lived on the bridge for three gloriously peaceful weeks. We got to know the kilometre-long cutting intimately, every tree, each blade of grass, and bird, whilst each of our photographic locations was given a name. Meals were taken on the grass alongside the Commer. We became good friends with a local farmer who brought his two cows onto the railway bank for grazing, and although we couldn't communicate verbally, we were kept well supplied with regular milk, eggs and fruit including the largest red cherries imaginable. Turtle doves purred in the lazy heat and the scratchy song of the whitethroat could always be heard. Quail called from the fields, green woodpeckers shrieked their strident 'yaffle' from a lineside coppice, whilst deer fed on a crop of young peas next to the bridge. We were in a rural paradise; fields of haystacks, huge carthorses, colourful fieldworkers – old women bent double and farm labourers like the rustic figures from Cézanne's 'Cardplayers'. And glimpses of Corot in the meandering brooks and willow

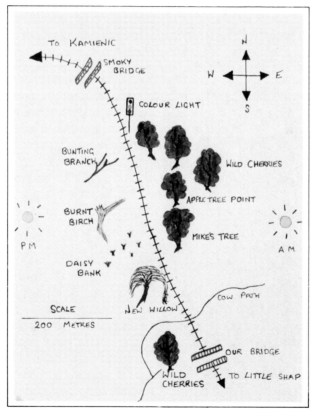

The names of our photographic locations at Bycen were all steeped in the lore of that amazing sojourn. Our favourite was Bunting Branch so named, because we found a baby corn bunting there.

trees backed by the orange-roofed houses of Byczen. Here was rural Poland, safe, peaceful and totally unspoilt.

Most evenings Eva's mother cooked for us, and we would spend a few contented hours with the family before returning to our bridge. When we didn't go to Eva's we would sit in the advancing twilight, listening to the owls. After dark a nightingale sang solely for us, and each night he lulled us to sleep with his soft melodies.

That enchanted place reminded me of childhood summers spent on the banks of steam main lines. The Pt 47s were fabulous; superbly maintained, clean and about the size of an LNER A2. Those we saw dated back to the early fifties. This extract from my notes reveals their magnificence:

Sunday, 19 June 1983

The Klodzko-Katowice express passed this evening in epic style; Pt 47 No 113 with lamps blazing and a massive roar of exhaust issuing a mighty cloud of grey smoke into the atmosphere. With steam spouting noisily from her cylinder cocks she burst under the bridge, totally enveloping us in smoke as the twelve coach train thundered beneath. The cutting was filled with smoke which hung in the air for minutes afterwards, sweet smelling and evocative in the pure evening air. The rain had, once again, made the atmosphere clear, amplifying the throbbing rhythms as the train receded through the wet countryside. Minutes later, a Ty 2 – a German war engine – came the other way and no sooner had it passed than a bunting began to sing a plaintive little song from the bushes by the path.

The midday express from Klodzko to Katowice bursts beneath 'our bridge' with Pt 47 No 113 in charge.

After two months we became immersed in Poland; it was tranquil, law-abiding and devoutly religious. The warmth of the people captivated us, even the tolerance of the authorities – notwithstanding that two weeks of our stay had been spent in negotiating in the capital. It was with a heavy heart that we left our enchanted bridge to return to the West German border, bound for the second stage of our adventure, Yugoslavia. No sooner were we back in the West than the quiet, reflective world of Poland evaporated. Everything glinted in the sun, everything went fast; big cars, huge lorries, endless motorways. The modernity of affluence around engulfed us in an instant.

Yugoslavia is not a member of the Warsaw Pact, but remains one of the hardest countries in the world for photographers. A camera on a beach in the Adriatic is fine, but when one tries to go 'up country' and photograph strategic military items like railways, then the whole weight of the establishment descends with a vengeance. I knew from my experience in 1972 that we had to obtain the right papers. So began the long process of negotiating with ministries, this time without the help of the BBC. Fortunately, Yugoslavia is split into six semi-autonomous socialist republics, so if one turned us down, we had recourse to another.

On arrival in Zagreb we visited the Minister of Transport to enquire about the historical classes of Hungarian extraction that were still working in Croatia. These types had been ceded to Yugoslavia following the carving up of the Austro-Hungarian Empire after World War I. One type I was particularly keen to document, was the class 22 Prairies. Long since finished in Hungary, the last survivors were working in Croatia. We were told only one remained in service, at Varaždin. Another type we were interested in was the 51 class 2-6-2T, the old Hungarian 375s. These were working from Karlovac and we were lucky enough to be given permission to make pictures of both types.

On my last abortive visit to Croatia in 1972 Varaždin had twenty of these Prairies for a network of secondary lines. Now only No 22024 remained. She was spotless. This puzzled us, and through an interpreter we asked why an engine on the point of withdrawal should be so resplendent. Apparently the engine was cleaned daily in deference to an historic type of which the men had been extremely fond. Railway enthusiasm is virtually unknown in Yugoslavia, yet the rank and file railwaymen have their own way of expressing sentiment. The fabulous night session that we did with this engine was in the nick of time for she was withdrawn two days later.

South of Zagreb, the modern Croatian city of Karlovac seemed an unlikely place to find vintage engines, but at the depot were three 51s looking very old, their design dating from the early years of the century. These were working passenger and mixed trains along the lightly laid crosscountry line to Sisak 102km away. The line had opened in 1893 and many of the rails were the originals. Only when the track is strengthened can diesels be considered. It seemed possible that the 51s had been on this route ever since its inception in 1907, and if so, eighty years of constant service on one route is a comparatively rare distinction. The line was truly rural; trains meandering through sleepy countryside, passing ungated level crossings; small wayside stations with sidings, goods sheds and beautifully tended gardens.

Unlike the 22 Prairie, the 51s were extremely drab, so we asked the area superintendent for permission to paint them with red trim, and though dumb-founded, he agreed. With adequate paint supplies in the Commer, we plied the length of the line from Karlovac to a halfway station called Vrginmost. A few miles from there was a fine location where the line climbed a steep bank, so we would wait in Vrginmost station for the afternoon passenger from Sisak. If the engine was dirty Maggie would leap into action as soon as the train stopped, paint brush in hand, whilst the station master asked the amazed crew to make smoke for us at an appointed spot on the bank. Then we would race the train to the bank and photograph the red-trimmed engine belching its pall of smoke before continuing the chase sixteen kilometres to Vojnić where there was a beautiful meadow full of purple flowers. This was a perfect spot for a wide-

Not content with painting the engines Maggie set about the water column at Vrginmost too!

angled lens picture of the train leaving the station on the final leg of the run to Karlovac.

Our attention now focussed on Serbia. This meant another journey down the Belgrade Highway. Although it was eleven years since I'd travelled it, it was little less disgusting. Slight improvements had been made; but there were still the burnt-out wrecks and photographs of the dead peeping out from the grass.

In Belgrade we talked with the Ministry of Transport about the most legendary of all Yugoslavian types, the 01 2-6-2s; a type of engine I'd dreamed about for twenty years and which I knew was working in Serbia.

These brilliant Prairies were originally the main line express engines for Serbia, and once worked from Zagreb to Belgrade and then to Niš in the south. Their duties included hauling the twice-weekly Orient Express. They are beautifully proportioned, and in their heyday watches were set by their impeccable timing.

Officials at the Ministry of Transport in Belgrade were reluctant to give us permission to go out in search of 01s. As fast as they said that one shed didn't have them, I came up with another which did. Then they decided that none was working so I asked if we could go and see one that was dead. No, they didn't think there was much point in that. After tremendous pressure from the British Embassy the authorities relented and said that they would produce an 01; it would be clean, in steam and we would be able to photograph it. But we would have to pay and wait one month. The month's waiting was secondary to the price, £1,500! Impossible!

Shattered by our failure with the 01s, I began negotiating for our last priority, the class 20s which worked the branch from Šid to Bijeljina. But the ministry was not prepared to give permission for these either. Demoralised, we determined to go to Šid and find someone who spoke English to accompany us to the local authorities. By incredible good fortune, the first person we stopped was a young Serb named Saša Milanovic. He spoke excellent English, was working for the regional radio station and, fascinated by our mission, suggested an interview! The next day I was on the air – with an interpreter – telling of the historical importance of the class 20s; how they were part of Germany's master-plan to dominate all territories from Berlin to Baghdad, following collusion with the Ottoman Empire. They were intended for use on the line from Turkey down into Arabia. This plan was thwarted, however, by the outbreak of the Balkan War. The Serbian army seized the 20s and used them for their war effort.

The interview proved to be the catalyst for our receiving authority to photograph on the line to Bijeljina, and in Šid's locomotive shed, where five class 20s were allocated. The type had been designed by Borsig of Berlin during that builder's preoccupation with English aesthetics, and the 20s had a distinct 'North Staffordshire' appearance.

We became good friends with the depot chief, a family friend of Saša's, and passed many happy days encamped in the shed yard. One evening Saša and the depot chief invited us out to dinner at a special restaurant outside Šid. It was a wonderful evening. A gipsy band in traditional costume played as we ate. I told of the remarkable changes I'd seen in Yugoslavia since my first visit; the increase in consumer goods, not least motor cars, and the general improvement in lifestyle. My comments pleased the chief greatly, as he was a member of the Communist Party. We talked railways, in depth, and he was under no illusions about the marvellous work that could be done with steam, foreseeing a time when oil would become increasingly expensive. He recalled times when men were on the footplate for twenty-four-hour stretches during the reconstruction of Yugoslavia after World War II. Throughout that traumatic time the 20s ran superbly, irrespective of maintenance. No diesel or electric could ever have survived such working conditions.

Maggie and I had now spent four months amongst steam locomotives; once again they had become a natural part of our daily routine. It was with foreboding that we headed northwards up the Belgrade Highway bound for the chromium-plated modernity of the West.

North Staffordshire in 1920? Rural joys at Visnjicevo as a Class 20 Mogul heads the afternoon passenger from Bijelina to Šid.

·16·
China – Four Momentous Visits

I stood entranced. The vast shop contained twenty boilers in various stages of construction; inner and outer fireboxes contrasted with boiler shells, all illuminated and silhouetted in ghostly patterns by the welders' blinding flashes, and set to a deafening cacophony of heavy drilling. The memories came flooding back – Crewe, Derby, Doncaster, Swindon – it mattered not. As if by magic I was back once more amid the vitality of the steam age, and it was every bit as fabulous as I remembered it to be.

That first trip to Datong, on the edge of Mongolia, fulfilled a burning ambition to witness the world's foremost steam locomotive plant. At the time of our visit, one JS Mikado was being produced every day as part of a special campaign. The Chinese have the intelligence to say, 'We have the coal; we have the water; and we have the labour. We can build a new steam locomotive for one eighth of the cost of a diesel. It will be equally reliable in service, and won't consume valuable oil reserves'.

The birth of a locomotive; an outer firebox at Datong Works.

The erecting shop at Datong. The cylinder block in the foreground is waiting to be lifted into place and the mighty overhead crane was driven by a teenage girl complete with plaits!

Sand moulds being dried by jets of flaming coal gas in the casting shop. When the sand is baked hard it is ready to receive the molten metal for making the wheels of a locomotive.

Early morning in the erecting shop saw a naked frame standing over the pits, and, during the course of the day, that frame would manifest into a fully-fledged locomotive. As we watched the drama with incredulity, our red-blooded Communist guide turned to me and said 'Our workers move like Charlie Chaplin did in your old movies'.

It had been a long struggle to get into China, where all kinds of exotic rarities were thought to exist. Back in the seventies I had sought help from former Prime Minister Edward Heath. We were both writing books for Sidgwick & Jackson at the time. He was one of the first world leaders to pioneer good relations with China and, receiving me at his home, he took an interest in my work. But nothing came of it; China at that time was irretrievably closed to the individual.

The break finally came when Gina Corrigan of Occidor, the China travel specialists, asked me to lead their railway tours. In order for me to research an itinerary, Gina obtained visas for Maggie and me, and in the winter of 1983 we set off for Manchuria – the best area for steam in China.

Landing at Beijing, we proceeded by internal flight to Harbin, capital of Heilongjiang Province in the far north-east. Christmas was only a few days away, and the temperature an incredible −25°C. Many of the visitors at our hotel, were from Hong Kong; dressed for the Arctic, they had come to experience snow and frost in China's coldest city.

Arrangements were made with our guide, Jin-Zhi-Yong, to visit Wanggang, ten miles south of Harbin on the main line to Peking. Decked in thermals, moon-boots, and with handwarmers glowing in our pockets, we watched the endless succession of heavy southbound freights climbing Wanggang bank; their billowing exhausts, issuing into deep blue sky, never seemed to evaporate. Colourfully embellished QJs and JS Mikados looked magnificent in a landscape dusted with snow. We were in ecstasy over the trains, but in agony over the temperature. The biting Manchurian wind cut our faces like a carving knife, ice gathered on our eyelashes, and our breath left frosty white patches on the cameras. Watery eyes made focussing difficult, and it was impossible to handle the equipment efficiently whilst wearing heavy gloves.

Four hours' exposure was all our systems could tolerate, and the cold soon sapped our concentration. Fortunately, there was a platelayers' hut at Wanggang where we could gain some respite from the cold, and much of Christmas was spent huddled around the small fire inside. But whatever our pictures lacked in mental application was more than compensated for by the sheer spectacle of the trains themselves.

After a week at Wanggang, Jin-Zhi-Yong took us to Sankong Bridge, over-looking the vast marshalling yard where the southbound trains are assembled. The yard was phenomenally busy, and including the JF Mikados on shunts, a steam train passed under the bridge every three minutes. The greatest drama was the departure of the double-headers. After a round of whistling, the cylinder cocks burst into action, and vast shrouds of steam haloed the QJs' blue, green and red fronts. Stars and other decorations gleamed in the sun as the giants departed like volcanoes on the move, drawing their 3,000 ton hauls with rhythmic stealth. Their exhausts rang sharply in the brittle atmosphere, creating a superb polyphony of rhythm. Upon passing under our bridge, the vast clouds of steam 'puthered' onto the road, bringing all traffic to a standstill until the engines were at least thirty wagon-lengths up the line.

Sankong Bridge is perhaps the greatest train-watching place on earth; Maggie and I were totally preoccupied. Jin-Zhi-Yong kept talking about the Ice Festival in Zhaolin Park, but neither of us was very interested, so great was the railway's allure. Finally he dragged us there; what a sight, it was the eighth wonder of the world! An exhibition of illuminated ice statues carved to lifesize from vast blocks of ice, taken from the Songhua River. Paddle-steamers, palaces, monuments and castles utterly dwarfed the spectators. A unique spectacle, and one of the most beautiful sights we had ever experienced. The festival opens on New Year's Day, and remains until the spring thaw in March.

'The Birdcage of adult life'. Sankong Bridge in Harbin with a brace of QJs pulling heavily out of the yards on a freight train half-a-mile long.

Our visit to Harbin ended with a traditional Chinese banquet, and amongst the local dishes was bear's paw, which I hasten to add we left for our hosts to enjoy. Before the meal I casually mentioned to our hosts that the world's first steam locomotive was built in Britain in 1804 and at the end of the repast, Mr Lou Binsheng – manager of the travel service – stood up, raised his glass and solemnly proposed a toast. And his proposal? The year 1804!

From Harbin, Maggie and I continued along the old South Manchurian main line to Shenyang, one of the oldest industrial towns in China. Sujatun sheds near Shenyang have an allocation of 110 steam locomotives, and pride of the depot was Pacific No 751, the last representative of China's 'streamlined' era of the thirties. She was one of twelve engines built in Japan for working the air-conditioned 'Asia Express', between the main towns of Manchuria and Dalian (Lüda) on the Yellow Sea Coast.

A railway museum was being put together at Shenyang, although it consisted of nothing more than a string of rusty engines on a siding. This was the only move towards railway preservation in China, but one day will doubtless develop into one of the finest railway collections in the world.

Only sixty-four kilometres from Shenyang was Anshan, a highspot of the tour. Our visit coincided with that of David Blunkett and his Sheffield City Councillors, who had arrived to twin the two cities. Appropriate, since Anshan produces an incredible fourteen million tons of iron and steel a year – a considerable percentage of Britain's national total from just one Chinese works! The Sheffield team was accompanied by Zhou Yongli, who became one of our closest friends. Originally a waiter, Zhou had struggled to learn English, and progressed through the China travel service. He spoke glowingly of the tremendous energy of Sheffield's blind leader.

Anshan works had forty steam locomotives assigned to internal service. Eight classes were present, principally Mikados and Prairies of fully-fledged proportions. But amongst the roster were several of the famous United States Army Transportation Corps (USATC) 0-6-0 shunting tanks, built in America for Allied operations during World War II.

We spent a lot of time in Anshan, not least in Steel Mill No 1 where a bank of flaming open-hearth furnaces reminded me of the words written by James Nasmyth, inventor of the steam hammer, following a visit he made to the Black Country in the 1830s. Nasmyth described 'Smut-covered, white-eyed men who dashed between the flames against a roaring cacophony of furnaces and clanging mills'. Here in front of our cameras seemed the essence of the Industrial Revolution.

When the furnaces are tapped, the waste flows down a separate channel into huge cauldron wagons standing below. Hour by hour we waited, trying to capture every facet of the drama with our cameras, for when the ladles are full, the locomotives come to convey the contents out to the periphery of the complex, whereupon the waste is tipped – still molten – down the slag bank. The flaming yellow liquid explodes in a cataclysmic blaze; crimson fingers pour from a molten river into every nook and cranny of the bank; and the searing heat can be felt several hundred metres away. These slag tips were my favourite of all Anshan's multifarious activities, a great industrial drama, now on the verge of extinction, and one which mirrored the days when Sheffield was at its industrial height and known as 'Hell with the lid off'.

After spending a week in the complex, Zhou suggested a trip southwards along the main line to a spot near Saddle Mountain where we could photograph the Shenyang to Dalian freights, with the mountain in the background. Upon arrival billowing shrouds of steam could be seen a mile away; a freight was approaching. But before the QJ had reached us, a second pall of steam appeared in the distance and not long after a third. This was repeated until eight trains had passed – one every five and a half minutes. It was definitive lineside photography, and Maggie and I were ecstatic. When it was time to leave, four hours later, no less than thirty southbound freights had passed that spot; QJs and JF Mikados, including several newly built at Datong works. 'Zhou', I said, 'you can't see this anywhere else on earth. This must be the busiest steam line in the world'. Sure enough, as we prepared to leave, two more plumes of steam were visible on the horizon.

Only forty-eight kilometres away was China's coal capital, Fushun, which provides much of the coal for Anshan works; Fushun has the world's biggest opencast mine, and it was on this network that we found another veteran from World War II, one of the famous USATC S160 2-8-0s.

Our final visit was to Tangshan, in the province of Hebei. Tangshan was known to be building steam locomotives during the early seventies, but on 8 July 1976, a massive earthquake ripped through the city, leaving the entire area in ruins and killing 148,000 people. Today, like a phoenix risen from the ashes, Tangshan is completely rebuilt.

The main north to south route through the city is called 'Construction Road'; a wide and modern thoroughfare, ten kilometres long, and lined with multi-storey dwellings. From Phoenix Hill, the sight of the newly built urban and industrial areas, stretching almost to the horizon, tells much of the indomitable spirit of the Chinese.

Once again Tangshan is producing two SY Mikados a week for use in coal mines, docks and iron and steel works. Over one thousand have now been built.

The short winter days melted into one another as Maggie and I became mesmerised by activities in Tangshan works. In the forges, piles of Anshan bars waited to be melted down for manufacture of detailed parts. We were reminded of James Nasmyth once again whilst watching the mighty, ground-shaking steam hammers convert huge oblong billets into the rounded driving axles for an SY.

In the castings shop, wheel moulds were dried by jets of flaming coal gas, before receiving molten metal. A huge ladle, borne on an overhead crane, moved from mould to mould, imbibing them with liquid steel, like the unceasing activities of a fertilising bee.

In the corner of the castings was a carbon converter; a demonic electric arc furnace which crackled, grunted and shot fire. At loading time the lid lifted to reveal four red-hot prongs, and it was fed with scrap and limestone by a bucket with a capsizing bottom, the meshing of which hung limply silhouetted against the converter's fiery incandescence like a giant sea squid.

We followed the progress of wheels and cylinders from rough castings on the sandy floor, to finished, burnished completion in the machine shops. The erecting shop held two SYs at a time, and although assembly was less avid than at Datong, the thrill of seeing an SY manifest from mere pieces in the finishing shop to a complete locomotive within three days, was unforgettable. Our tour was drawing to a close, and we returned to Beijing, enchanted by all we had seen.

Tienamen Square in the heart of Peking reveals the cleanliness, orderliness and discipline which characterises Chinese society. A portrait of the national hero Chairman Mao can be seen presiding over the entrance to the Forbidden City.

Visitors flock to the Yungang Buddhist Caves, one of the most remarkable grottos on earth and only eight miles from Datong Locomotive Works.

China's railways are the lifeline of her economy, and thirteen new lines are currently under construction. There are no motorways, no juggernauts, and few family cars; because there is no need for them. It was evident to us that this coherent transport policy was a cornerstone of China's social stability. Free from rabid road development, and all accompanying social tensions.

The success of that memorable tour led to our subsequent visits with the Occidor group each September when, in addition to the railway, we take them to many of China's great cultural attractions; the Forbidden City in Beijing, preserved as the seat of China's Imperial Emperors over many centuries; the monumental Great Wall, spanning some of the most inhospitable terrain on earth; and the Buddhist Caves at Yungang where 50,000 Buddhist statues are enshrined in an incredible cliff-face grotto.

But the highspot of our Occidor tour is a final unforgettable day on Wanggang bank. We arrive early morning and set up close to the summit to enjoy a full day's action photography. A constant succession of steam-hauled trains has for every group engendered an elixir of youth, as for a short time the enthusiasm of childhood summers lives again.

An on-location coffee stall is set up, and the ladies of the party – apart from taking pictures – prepare a superb buffet lunch. It is a day of great companionship, marvellous trains, and brilliant photography. In the evening, as the sun sinks, we leave the grassy banks and trudge across the fields to our coach which will take us back to Harbin and a grand farewell dinner.

China exemplifies the validity of a railway economy; her steam fleet is 10,000 strong – a third of the world's active total – and developments in steam traction continue. After building the QJ, fundamentally unchanged for thirty years, plans are now in hand for new designs. David Wardale, the British engineer who achieved worldwide recognition building the 'Red Devil' for South Africa's railways, is now permanently at Datong under contract on development work. China's aim for a 20 per cent thermal efficiency is now recognised as nothing more than a political ideal. Yet much work can be done with the conventional steam locomotive, and it is heartening to know that a British engineer should be in permanent residence in this last great shrine of steam.

China has also offered consultancy work to 150 middle-aged engineers redundant from British Rail's Doncaster Works. The Chinese are wise people; they recognise the value of British engineering skills and wish to utilise them in their railway development.

The Chinese are not just perpetuating the age of steam, but more important, the age of railways. These are the people who could now teach us, the British, the proper role of a railway in a modern economy.

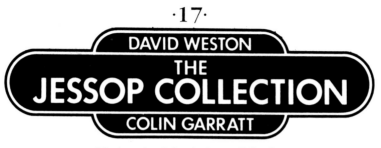

DAVID WESTON
THE
JESSOP COLLECTION
COLIN GARRATT

The letterhead for the Jessop Collection.

In 1969, a self-employed picture framer was given the chance to realise his dream of making a living from painting. On the other side of the city, a successful sales manager for a wholesale grocery company handed in his notice to begin the impossible task of documenting the last steam locomotives of the world. At the same time, the city council was drawing up plans for the building of a huge underpass next to a small but popular photographic retailer. It was the beginning of a Leicester success story.

'You must go and see that bloke who sits in his shop window and paints – he does a lot of trains'. If I heard this once, I heard it a thousand times, until curiosity got the better of me and I went along to see what the fuss was about. Sure enough, in his little picture-framing shop next to the railway, David Weston was sitting at his easel, taking his first venture into the unknown.

We related well to each other; David was not convinced that he would survive, and didn't think I had much chance, either. His cynicism was well founded, having spent years trying to get his work acknowledged. With a wife and young daughter to support, he had suffered the demoralisation of one rejection after another, and was so desperate for money that he had to resort to painting local beauty spots on cards with calendar tabs and selling them door to door. He was very close to giving up when he received his first 'break', a three-month exhibition at the British Transport Museum granted him by the curator, the late John Scholes. He was working on the pictures at the time of my visit.

I knew nothing about art, and David's paintings were the first I had ever been confronted with. I was overawed by them. Equally, David liked my work and we noticed a similarity in style. He was especially attracted to a picture of mine depicting two Stanier 8Fs photographed through a smashed window at Newton Heath. It was a compliment to me that he painted this scene and hung the picture in his shop and next time I visited him the painting had been sold.

As my career advanced, I never found time to go back, and it was to be sixteen years before I saw David again. During that time we followed each other's careers with interest. I had seen David's 'Weston Collection' as it toured the country, and I observed that his painting had become infinitely more skilled, and knew that his canvases were attracting handsome sums of money. Equally, David had seen articles about me in the national press and magazines, and had noticed my books as they came out every year, along with reviews of our AV shows. He knew that the seemingly impossible task of documenting the last steam locomotives of the world was not only going ahead, but dramatically so.

Visiting David at the 'Lazy Acre' all those years later, his success was evident; a superb showman's wagon graced his lawn with an elegant new picture gallery nearby – 'I once had six millionaires on this lawn at the same time', David joked. We passed into the studio furnished with Victorian decor and as I stood alongside his easel the clock seemed to slip back a century.

Afterwards sitting by the fireside in his beautiful home, we reflected on our feelings of trepidation in 1969. At the end of a delightful evening, David suddenly smiled and said 'Right then, Colin, what shall we do together?' I was delighted for he echoed my own sentiments. The obvious project was an exhibition, but David, ever practical, was quick to point out the cost of mounting a national touring exhibition. The logistics of keeping and maintaining such an enterprise would be considerable. We would need backing, preferably from someone who had related interests. It didn't take long to decide on the ideal person to approach.

Alan Jessop is managing director of the Leicester-based photographic company, whose success over recent years has been phenomenal. What began as a one-man shop in a Leicester high street, opened by Alan's father Frank in 1930, has now become one of the biggest names in photographic retailing. Jessop's was 'the first company to send cameras through the post', and although development of that underpass caused the loss of much trade, mail order increased and the company moved to larger premises. It was a big step, and one which earned a mention in the *Guinness Book of Records* as the new building had a floor space of 27,000sq ft, and had become famous as 'the world's biggest photographic store'. Large stocks, fast service, but above all, the keenest prices, made Jessop's a household name, and the company has forty branches nationwide.

Alan recognised the potential of a joint exhibition immediately, and jumped at the chance of being able to put something back into photography in such a unique way. The subject matter is perfect; he is an ex-trainspotter, and takes an interest in industrial history. But his involvement was no better justified than when he said, 'I just like the pictures!'

The fact that a photographer is seen by a successful artist to have achieved a comparable lucidity of expression, is, for the photographer, a mark of high rank. Indeed, as Alan Jessop himself observed, 'It is unusual for the two disciplines to unite in such close collaboration'. Yet David and I have reached similar conclusions by striving to portray the 'atmosphere' of the subject. David

Three generations of Jessops at the company's new computerised distribution centre in Leicester. Left to Right: Frank Jessop, Alan Jessop and Christopher Jessop.

A happy moment in David Weston's studio as we review progress on David's paintings for the Jessop Collection.

had long been preoccupied with the majesty of steam, and its decline was, in his own words, 'The final chapter in the story of one of mankind's greatest inventions'.

David and I experience this awareness with similar emotions. Thus treatment of such elements as rust, grease, light and nuance of colour closely resembles each other's, indeed uncannily so. This was evident when examining the exhibition pictures. My photograph of a Greek scrapyard bore a remarkable similarity to David's painting of a scene at Cohen's scrapyard in Kettering. The style and composition of the two images were almost the same. Excitedly, we came to another strange conclusion, that it was difficult to distinguish – from a short distance – whether the pictures were paintings or photographs.

When overseas, I often think of David sitting cosily at his easel whilst I go to the ends of the earth to make my pictures. If I compose a snow scene I have to stand in it – probably for hours on end, whilst the painter's snowscapes come from the comfort of his fireside. Yet the painter's grappling for perfection is little easier than the photographer's; if David achieves six masterpieces a year he is doing well and the same for me as a photographer. But the painting gains in monetary value; a fine David Weston canvas is worth several thousand pounds and will probably be sold before it is completed, whereas an image on a colour transparency has little intrinsic value and even when made into a print will be worth only a few pounds. But paradoxically photography is regarded more seriously in the longer term; the photograph being seen as the reality – the essence of time and event.

It is contrasts such as these which constitute a fascinating adjunct to the Jessop Collection and add an intellectual dimension to the voluptuousness of the scenes.

As an indication of the impact that David's pictures exert upon me I recount an uncanny incident regarding his canvas of two Robinson GC Director 4-4-0s standing side by side in the gloomy depths of Leicester Central shed. The two engines, decked in green livery with red trim, are doused in glorious potions of sunlight, smoke and shadow against the shadowy depths of the shed interior. David himself is too young to have ever witnessed this, and had done the picture from references, but I knew that exactly such scenes had taken place there on countless occasions and the potent imagery compelled me to visit the spot where it had occurred. The fact that the Great Central Shed no longer exists – the site now being a private woodyard – was irrelevant. I simply clambered over the fence in order to stand physically in the timespace of that mystical vision.

The Jessop Collection is due to launch in the winter season of 1987/8. It will be a Leicester success story; the coming together of three local lads in the creation of a wonderful visual experience – the result of a fateful day in 1969 when I went to see 'that bloke who paints trains'!

·18·
The Gold Coast

Vast tracts of fever-laden jungles had to be penetrated by British engineers to build the Gold Coast's first railway. The coast is hemmed in by a belt of jungle 240 kilometres deep and to hack through this rain forest interspersed with mosquito-infested pools and swamps demanded unbelievable determination. Malaria was rife; many died of disease, others went raving mad. But if the huge reserves of gold in the interior were to be exploited a railway had to be constructed.

Beginning at the coastal village of Sekondi in 1899, the line progressively embraced the communities at Tarkwa, Dunkwa, Obuasi, and in September 1903 it reached the Ashanti kingdom of Kumasi, an incredible 265 kilometres inland.

Extensions to the network made the Gold Coast Railways the pride of Africa. Apart from opening up the goldfields, the railway developed Ghana's vast potential for cocoa, to found the Cadbury empire, whilst manganese from Nsuta, bauxite from Awaso, and timber from Kumasi, all flowed down the West line to the coast for export.

Passenger travel was luxurious; within two decades of the dark country being opened up, trains with restaurant and sleeping facilities were in service, and travellers could assuage their thirst with a bottle of Bass for sixpence, or whisky and soda for ninepence. Truly the advance of civilisation!

Upon arrival in Accra in May 1985 to tour the system, I was welcomed by Sue Buckwell from the British Council. I was shocked when she told me the state Ghana Railways were in. I knew there were problems, but the decline was more serious than I imagined; not only were there no steam locomotives in service, but, far worse, hardly any trains were running at all. Years of neglect and a constant shortage of foreign exchange for spares, combined with unrestricted importation of articulated lorries by private transport operators, had reduced the railway to a wreck. This prevented Ghana from moving her heavy commodities to the coast for export. Only gold was being exported freely – a commodity not dependent on the railway.

Familiar feelings of anger welled up yet again; another once magnificent railway system gone to rack and ruin. I thought of the enormous capacity at home – both in terms of industrial plant, and skilled manpower – that could and should be used, and the need for dialogue and liaison.

A visit to the railway in Accra confirmed what Sue had said. The station had blistering woodwork and an aura of decay. The huge marshalling yards had been turned into a fruit and vegetable market, the railway's only passenger traffic being market women who came from the countryside to sell their produce in Accra. Sidings were rusty and unused, one spluttering diesel stood smokily in the depot yard, whilst the shed itself was full of dead steam locomotives, none of which had turned a wheel in months, as the Indian experts who run the railway have forbidden the use of steam. Bruce Tagoe, the loco foreman, was a railwayman down to his fingertips, Bruce had been trained at the Vulcan Foundry; he sat pondering on the failed diesels and his inability to use his steam locomotives to maintain a minimal service.

While in Accra I was invited to stay with Michael Bottomley, the Managing Director of the Ashanti Gold Corporation, a joint government and Lonhro operation which operated Ghana's biggest gold mine at Obuasi. I was well cared for with the help of his wife Pam and their marvellous house staff. The name of their house was 'Villa Rose' and each morning a fresh rose from the garden would be placed on my tray of coffee. I was alone as Maggie – exhausted after an arduous AV season – had work to do at the cottage.

Michael, along with the help of S. S. Nayak, the Indian General Manager of Ghana Railways, helped formulate an itinerary that would embrace the principal industries served by the railway. First I would travel along the coast to Takoradi, which was close to Location where the railway works and HQ were situated. Thence to Tarkwa to visit the huge manganese mines at Nsuta before proceeding to Ghana Bauxite at Awaso. A visit to the Ashanti Gold Mine at Awaso would follow before reaching Kumasi.

I had desperately wanted to travel by rail but the unreliability of trains – if they ran at all between Accra and Takoradi – forbade this and arrangements were made for a Land-Rover and driver to accompany me as far as Kumasi.

The road from Accra to Takoradi follows the coast, and passes many of the old forts from which slaves were taken to America and the Caribbean until the trade was prohibited by the British in 1807. Elmina Castle, perched high above the billowing ocean, retained all the atmosphere of its former horrors, as the roar of the ocean echoed through its abandoned walls. I went below into the holding dungeons, still pervaded by an overpowering sense of evil. I saw the hole through which the slaves were pushed, one by one, to slither down a chain into the waiting ship far below. Many of the slaves were sold to Dutch and Portuguese traders by the Ashantis for this vile trade was not just the activity of the white man.

Along the coast, Britain's former presence remained evident; advertisements for Milo, Bournvita, Ideal Milk, and Omo, whilst Ghana's post boxes were red, with Elizabeth R embossed on their sides. All radio announcements begin with 'This is the GBC,' (Ghana Broadcasting Corporation). English is the national

Elmina Castle. Visiting these old slaving forts was of particular significance as it was in such places as this that the ancestors of the great negro jazzmen were held prior to being shipped to America.

language, having superseded the various tribal tongues.

After independence, Ghana was the most developed of all African nations and was widely tipped to have a bountiful future. Tragically, corruption in high places destroyed the economy and at one stage brought the country to the edge of famine.

Now Ghana is struggling to recover from the chaos under the firm leadership of Flight Lieutenant Jerry Rawlings. Tremendous progress is being made but difficulties remain and typical of the good natured Ghanaians, problems are referred to as 'Ghana palaver'. Whenever anything goes wrong, one never loses one's temper, or even tries to apportion blame, but simply puts it down to 'Ghana palaver'.

In Takoradi I stayed at the Railway Guest House, an English-styled residence of thirties vintage, complete with terrace overlooking the ocean. During my stay a perfect example of 'Ghana palaver' occurred when I said to Esa, the housekeeper: 'I hear you have a shortage of beer in Ghana'. 'Oh no, sir', he said, 'there is no shortage of beer in Ghana'. 'But Esa', I answered, 'you can't buy beer anywhere!' 'No, sir', he replied seriously, 'there is no shortage of beer, there is a shortage of bottles'.

Nameplates lying in the stores at Location sum up that Anglo-Ghanaian heritage as former Governors vie with local tribes, slaving forts and Ghanaian towns.

Volunteers turn out at weekends in a desperate attempt to repair the west line from Takoradi to Kamasi – the principal route for Ghana's heavy exports.

Location works was like a piece of industrial Lancashire grafted onto primeval forest. The shops had been well equipped despite much machinery having had to be shipped in duplicate due to losses from the surfboats. The yard was littered with derelict locomotives. I spoke with Mr Nyadro, the superintendent; he had the men to get the steam engines running but he'd been instructed not to do so. The spares required for diesels are very complex and he gave an instance of how a fault in a simple oil seal had stopped a complete locomotive because the oil was being flung over the radiator causing overheating. 'The simplest of all things', he said, 'but we can't get it'.

I spent many days in that historical works, once a vast British infrastructure that had transformed Ghana's wilderness into a place of prosperity and promise. As Mr Nyadro succinctly put it, 'We still look to Britain for guidance – the child may have grown up, but it still needs the guiding hand of its mother'.

Moving onto Tarkwa I visited the gangs of volunteers attempting – with the aid of a World Bank Loan – to renovate the West line. Their work songs were fascinating and included a call of response theme: 'Ghana Railway Rehabilitation! Ghana Railway Rehabilitation!'

Operations at the nearby manganese mines in Nsuta were worked by Ruston diesels, but in the shed yard stood their predecessors, a pair of Orenstein and Koppel's classic well tanks, whilst at the back of the shed was a magnificent Bagnall 2-6-2 tank, No 13. She was enormous; I had never seen a larger engine on 2ft 6in gauge.

No railway exists within the bauxite mines at Awaso but the washery feeds the ore into hoppers from which the twenty-ton rail wagons are filled for conveyance to the coast at Takoradi. Awaso's station master was a particularly unhappy man as he was forbidden to use his Hunslet 0-6-0 shunting tank – recently ex-works from Location. 'What do I shunt the yard with?' he asked. 'We are receiving cocoa, bauxite and timber but I have no shunting engine. When Location sends a diesel, it always breaks down'. He was equally frustrated about the shortage of wagons, one of his aides having undertaken a 112km walk from Awaso, only to discover eighty derailed or dumped bauxite wagons. 'The railway promises to retrieve them, but they never do', he explained. Of the 158 wagons allocated for bauxite only fifty-eight were in service.

At the bauxite mine I found the old RAF instruction huts and typical World War II explosives magazines, the bauxite having been vital for production of Spitfires and Hurricanes and Beyer Peacock sent six Garratts to work the heavy hauls to Takoradi.

Awaso's bauxite now goes to British Alcan at Burntisland in Fife. Alcan wish to increase production as Awaso's bauxite has a high aluminium content, but two shiploads a year are all the railway can manage, whilst a massive stockpile lies in the jungle awaiting conveyance.

My next stop was the Ashanti Gold Mine at Obuasi but on the way we called

Waiting to enter the cage one mile below ground in the Adansi shaft of the Ashanti Gold Mine.

at Dunkwa to visit the engine shed. It was characterised by the usual derelicts, including an original Vulcan Foundry 4-8-2 of 1923. I spent a fascinating hour with the depot foreman, talking about the days when the Garratts carried the bauxite. When working hard on an up-gradient, the fireman had to feed the firebox ten shovelfuls of coal every minute. 'We used to call them mankillers', he said, 'some of the firemen were so frightened of them that they got themselves transferred to other depots'.

Darkness fell as we sped on to Obuasi. On arrival I was hustled up to the huge canteen for a supper of cold beef and salad before being taken to my quarters. The next day, donning a light overall, heavy boots and helmet, I was taken into the mines. We entered a cage that carried us almost two kilometres down into the bowels of the earth where the heat and humidity were overpowering. My purpose was to photograph battery locomotives hauling gold ore from the cutting areas up to the shaft, but upon taking my camera from its case it misted over in an instant. Then came a wave of nausea; unable to breathe, I almost blacked out so intense was the humidity.

After walking a labyrinth of tunnels we reached the loading area. I had recovered and the camera lens had acclimatised and a marvellous sequence of pictures was made depicting workers digging the ore and the loaded trains departing. Upon emerging from those subterranean depths it was strange to feel the chill air of tropical Ghana!

Obuasi has one surface line which runs out into the bush to collect wood for use in the furnaces and as pit props. It is worked by Clayton diesels, but the old steam fleet apparently lay abandoned out in the bush and although several days were spent searching it was never found.

Further north at Kumasi eleven locomotives stood in various stages of decay – several reduced to frames only, with the nameplates still attached. At the side of the depot lay the fragmented remains of Vulcan 4-8-2 No 123, *Prince of Wales*. Realising that the nameplate was cast aside for scrap, I asked the foreman, Mr Sai, if I could take it, and with the general manager's permission he agreed. I've never been a collector of railwayana, but this proud engine epitomised its Anglo-Ghanaian heritage. Everywhere I looked were artifacts from Britain's days as the 'workshop of the world'; machine tools from Summerskill of Sowerby Bridge, and Smiths of Glasgow; anvils from Brooks of Lye; and clocks from Gents of Leicester, to name but a few.

Ghana has found nothing yet to match the reliability of her Vulcan Foundry long-boilered goods now going to the scrapyard decked in their British glory.

175

On the bus journey back to Accra an incident occurred which gave further insight into the Ghanaian's marvellous temperament. Our driver ignored a stop signal from a group of policemen monitoring traffic. Within seconds two police motorcyclists chased us and stopped the bus. Both policemen, fully armed, sauntered menacingly towards us. The passengers enjoyed this. 'It's de fuzz!' they roared, clapping loudly. One policeman was especially angry with the driver. 'Look at de big sulky boy!' a passenger gibed, 'he's cross because we didn't stop!' This was beginning to look nasty. Then a third officer followed by car; it was the sergeant and he carried an automatic rifle! Now the passengers really took off in gay abandon. 'Here come de big man! Watch out, fellas, here come your boss – straighten your helmet!' 'Bang bang, big man! You're dead!' I was terrified; the police were being provoked unmercifully. 'Any minute now', I thought, 'trouble will break out'. But the Ghanaians are sophisticated people; the police kept their cool simply telling the driver to reverse back to the checkpoint; they would search everyone's luggage. So the police got their revenge, and only when every case had been examined, were we allowed to continue. As we set off again, a smiling black face in the opposite seat asked 'How you like our country?'

Six hours later I arrived at the Bottomleys', and although they were away, the house staff welcomed me. My shoes were removed to be cleaned, the laundry boy followed me upstairs to take my washing whilst the houseboy brought a tray of coffee – complete with rose – and asked what time I would like dinner.

That evening at ten o'clock, the phone rang. It was Sue Buckwell; 'I heard you were getting back today, there's a farewell party being held in your honour tomorrow at my residence. Most of the people you have met in Accra are coming, including the British High Commissioner'. Sue put on a magnificent buffet and I felt proud to have been the catalyst in bringing so many eminent people together in the name of railways, and fervently hoped that the cross fertilisation that evening would bring some positive results.

The following evening I left the Bottomleys' for the airport. I was leaving a beautiful country that had hit an alltime low and was trying to regain stability. That stability partly depended on the railway, and I thought again of Britain's capacity to help. I thought of Rudyard Kipling's words 'And what should they know of England, who only England know?' The greatness of Britain's past achievements can only be seen from a global perspective. The Ghanaians have taken much from British culture, their institutions being modelled on those of the Mother country; but the railway, perhaps the greatest asset of all, has been forgotten.

I drove through the gates of the Villa Rose and headed for the airport. I didn't have to wonder whether the Ghana Airways 727 was the same plane that I'd flown out on two months earlier. I knew it was, for Ghana Airways has only one international jet.

It was shortly after dawn when we arrived at London Heathrow. Wrapped in dreams I waited for the cases to come along the conveyor belt in the baggege hall. There were two of them. No, there was a third; there it was, packed in plywood. I grabbed it and it struck the trolley with a crash. *Prince of Wales*, the dream was real. Long live that Anglo-Ghanaian heritage!

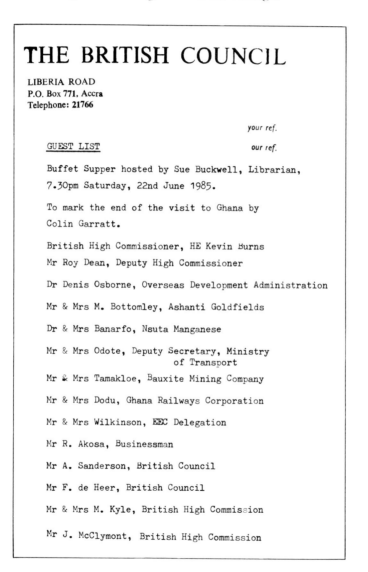

THE BRITISH COUNCIL

LIBERIA ROAD
P.O. Box 771, Accra
Telephone: 21766

your ref.

GUEST LIST   *our ref.*

Buffet Supper hosted by Sue Buckwell, Librarian,
7.30pm Saturday, 22nd June 1985.

To mark the end of the visit to Ghana by
Colin Garratt.

British High Commissioner, HE Kevin Burns

Mr Roy Dean, Deputy High Commissioner

Dr Denis Osborne, Overseas Development Administration

Mr & Mrs M. Bottomley, Ashanti Goldfields

Dr & Mrs Banarfo, Nsuta Manganese

Mr & Mrs Odote, Deputy Secretary, Ministry
                              of Transport

Mr & Mrs Tamakloe, Bauxite Mining Company

Mr & Mrs Dodu, Ghana Railways Corporation

Mr & Mrs Wilkinson, EEC Delegation

Mr R. Akosa, Businessman

Mr A. Sanderson, British Council

Mr F. de Heer, British Council

Mr & Mrs M. Kyle, British High Commission

Mr J. McClymont, British High Commission

Sue Buckwell's guest list for that memorable evening indicates the tremendous potential which exists for liaison between British industry and the railways of the developing world.

·19·
A Call to Arms

INTERNATIONAL
RAILWAY
FORUM

My dream is for the 'Forum' to become as well constituted as the TUC's Transport House.

Having been closely associated with railways for forty years – twenty of them professionally – what have I learnt? What conclusions have been reached? The most important is that mass transportation by road is uneconomic, undisciplined and anti-social.

One person every ninety minutes dies on Britain's roads. Consider the inexperienced seventeen year old; the angry husband who has rowed with his wife; or the drunkard. All three can get into their vehicles and travel at twice the legal speed, aiming these missiles in any direction. And they do; daily. The nation pays heavily for police, courts, fire brigade and hospitalisation. But no price can be put upon the pain and grief caused by this horrific maiming and loss of life.

Road building, maintenance, policing and transport, cost this country billions of pounds every year, whilst the price paid by our environment is beyond calculation. Meanwhile, the railway – a properly controlled transport system, once our greatest national asset – has been undermined and discarded. For three out of the last twenty years, not a single passenger has been killed on British Railways, but the railway's long tradition of quality service and reliability has been destroyed in the name of smalltime haulage operations, whilst the instincts of macho-man in his snazzy car are conditioned by TV commercials every thirty minutes.

We cannot expect those outside the railway community to support the industry's interests, unless they are provided with a positive and tangible incentive for doing so. The indictment against those who are supposed to care for railways is extremely serious:

Railway Management
Top management has consistently failed to convey to the nation the inherent value of railways, and the case for their retention and regeneration.

Railway Unions
Railway trade unions are under constant risk of manipulation by political agitators who have no inherent interest in the industry. The strike of 1982 served to illustrate, for the first time in 150 years, that Britain could sustain industrially and commercially without a railway, (albeit in the short term). Sure enough, within twelve months, Serpell tried to prove it in figures.

The Railway Press
Britain's railway press has presided shamefully over the demise of the industry, without addressing the burning issues which threaten the survival of railways. Editors have abdicated their responsibility to use position and specialised knowledge to further the case for railways.

The National Railway Museum
The pioneering of British-built railways across the world was at the very core of our unique industrial history. But our National Museum in York has failed to uphold this, by concentrating on our indigenous heritage, a policy contrary to its official remit. This presents a seriously distorted picture of the nation's railway legacy.

The Railway Enthusiasts
Millions of Britons are interested in railways. A wealth of specialised knowledge exists – as the ability of enthusiasts to run preserved railways proves. But these valuable members of the railway community are failing to speak out in a co-ordinated way against the industry's decline. Neither are they taking any positive interest in the needs of railways overseas. Enthusiasts' activities are invariably parochial and steeped in nostalgia. The extent of this nostalgia is indicated by the present Settle–Carlisle campaign; a pretty, romantic route? Of course; but why the national furore? When the vast marshalling yard at Carlisle – Kingmoor – was ripped up, and thousands of tons of Anglo/Scottish freight dumped onto the M6, no one blinked!

The Railwaymen
The rank and file railwaymen have witnessed the industry's decline with despair, and are thoroughly demoralised. Any military strategist knows that demoralisation is the natural harbinger of defeat. For the first time in history, the railwaymen have no solutions.

Throughout the entire railway movement, defeat is rife in apathy; and those with vested interests in other forms of transport are exceedingly pleased.

The Solution

A National Railway Forum must be instituted to promote railways, *past, present* and *future*. That forum to be comprised of able personages drawn from all aspects of the railway sphere; management, unions, industry, press and enthusiasts. The forum's national executive would preside over three distinct areas of action:

1 Proper Utilisation of Britain's Home Railway

The short-selling of railways must stop. Our railways have the potential to be the most economic and environmentally desirable form of transportation, and their case must be promoted to the public at large.

Many outside the railway sphere want action taken.

Sixty-ton juggernauts, with all their hideous inefficiency and environmental deprivation, charging along our highways at 120km/h, is no way to conduct a transport system. Neither are overcrowded motorways – deathtraps in anyone's language.

Government must be educated to the formulation of a properly co-ordinated transport policy, embracing investment to restore our railways and connect them with all relevant industries.

2 Co-ordination of Foreign Railways and British Manufacturers

The needs of foreign railways must be communicated to British manufacturers and government. Britain possesses the history, workshop capacity, engineering skills and inherent understanding of railways to fulfil this vital role. The work recently done by Hugh Phillips & Co in Tredegar on Sudanese locomotives is a perfect example of what is achievable.

The case for railways.

The rejuvenation of important railways, wherever they are, is a top priority. A co-ordinating body would facilitate this, in addition to campaigning for a reasonable percentage of government overseas aid to go to railways.

My visits to Ghana and Sudan, have already illustrated the necessity of such a body. In 1982 I emphasised strongly the need for spare parts, substantiated by a message from Sudan's Minister of Transport urgently requesting aid. In the same vein I was approached by a Moslem leader who had access to funds from Mecca that might be used for railway rejuvenation in Moslem lands. But there was no relevant organisation to which representations could be made.

If action had been taken over the needs of Sudan in 1982, the famine in the Darfur would almost certainly have been eased. But it took Band Aid to begin renovating the railway, a job which the railway community should have undertaken itself.

3 Worldwide Preservation of the Railway Heritage
Britain's role as railway builder to the world makes her the natural country to assist other nations in the accumulation of collections for future museums. Many countries would greatly welcome our help in this respect.

A natural adjunct of this work would be to select artifacts for repatriation, and eventual display in a much needed overseas heritage museum to offset the deficiency of our National Museum in York.

Once established, the forum's manifesto would be put to the country for support and donations would be drawn from private membership along with organisations and industries who supported its aims (as does the National Trust). Sponsorship of MPs with a declared interest in the railway industry would be an important long-term objective. After constitution, sub-divisions would be founded as outlined in (1), (2) and (3) above, each with a presiding executive.

I refrain from going into further detail; that is for wider consideration. I merely set out the framework for a forum, to embrace railway interests on all fronts. An impossible task? Of course it isn't! Railways have always been Herculean undertakings carried through with determination and temerity by dedicated men. Far from being a dying and outmoded industry, the challenges facing railways today are as exciting as they were in the 1840s.

United action is essential to offset the monumental tragedy that has befallen the railway industry over the last thirty years. The initiative must come from Britain; apart from her industrial base and historical perspective, sufficient Britons care about railways to provide the initial impetus. Those involved with railways are the *custodians of the heritage* in their time. To ignore the challenge is to engender disservice to oneself and country.

·20·
Tomorrow

What of tomorrow? In the last twenty years some fifty countries have been covered, twenty books written, television films and videos made, a fourth – even more spectacular – AV show is about to tour the nation, and our priceless picture collection is increasing all the time.

Yet, so vast is the heritage at stake that the work has hardly begun!

As my organisation grows so does the rate at which the steam age is ending. Financial investment from outside is now vital if the work is to be completed. The team is formed, ready and able to do justice to this dying epoch. It would be tragic if that team were dissipated through lack of funds. We now look to the country for support. We are not necessarily talking about large sums of money, as modest donations carefully deployed would enable valuable work to be done. Any investment would rapidly bring many times its value as this book has already proved. Apart from financing the expeditions we are fighting a rearguard action to computerise the most important pictures and so preserve them for posterity.

Every day of every week, of every year, locomotives, rolling stock, archives and entire railway networks are vanishing from the face of the earth. But I am forced to spend sixty per cent of each year raising funds. Having come this far, the work must be completed, for, although the steam locomotive will outlive me, most of the heritage will not survive the turn of the century and once it is gone it will never – but never – come back. To fail at this stage would be a tragedy, depriving future generations of an incomparable glimpse of a legendary age.

The strength of my legacy lies in its diversity; historically, geographically and artistically. Only a *comprehensive* pictorial collection will be of *intrinsic* value for the future. Tomorrow's technology will see production possibilities beyond imagination, and the images amassed by the end of the century, computerised for posterity in all their historical radiance, will constitute a matchless legacy. Imagine the reaction in a thousand years' time; it is for these unborn generations that my work is now devoted. We owe it to them.

I will continue to call for the National Railway Forum – both from the stage, and in all my published works – in the faith that tomorrow the initiative will be

My parents now form a vital part of the team; Dad controls finance and marketing with mum as his full time secretary.

(Lower left:) *Monica, theatrical, artistic and canny has handled every lecture/show booking I have ever done. Without her unfailing support I may not have survived.*

A milestone was reached in February 1978 when Alena Burton joined the organisation in charge of publishing, publicity and general promotions. Alena's 'laser beam' intellect has been one of our greatest assets ever since.

Maggie – 'The jewel in the crown'. Apart from being curator of the collection, Maggie handles picture presentations and design for books and magazines. Here we fulfil another aspect of our work by taking railways to generations 'born out of time'. Grace Dieu Prep School. (Coalville Times)

taken and the potential of such a body realised. The making of a definitive television documentary on my work over the last twenty years would be a positive step towards the forum and this is another hope for tomorrow.

Yes, the steam age will outlive me, but railways have traditionally taken their strength from continuity of service – sons following proudly in their fathers' footsteps – producing a stability which has been the bedrock of the industry's service to the nation. And so it was with that anticipation that the beginning of 1987 heralded the news that Maggie was bearing our first child, who, at the very time this book is published, should be born within sight of that Victorian bridge in the soft Leicestershire countryside.